This will be great if
we can train her.
After Lost week we need to
up the anti!
Happy Christmas Boo 2021
    X X X X.

SHEEPDOG TRAINING
and Trials

A COMPLETE GUIDE FOR
BORDER COLLIE HANDLERS AND ENTHUSIASTS

SHEEPDOG TRAINING
and Trials

A COMPLETE GUIDE FOR
BORDER COLLIE HANDLERS AND ENTHUSIASTS

Nij Vyas

THE CROWOOD PRESS

First published in 2010 by
The Crowood Press Ltd
Ramsbury, Marlborough
Wiltshire SN8 2HR

enquiries@crowood.com

www.crowood.com

This impression 2021

British Library Cataloguing-in-Publication Data
A catalogue record for this book is available from the British Library.

ISBN 978 1 84797 190 6

Disclaimer
The author and the publisher do not accept any responsibility in any manner
whatsoever for any error or omission, or any loss, damage, injury, adverse outcome,
or liability of any kind incurred as a result of the use of any of the information
contained in this book, or reliance upon it. If in doubt about any aspect of
sheepdog training or trials readers are advised to seek professional advice.

Line drawings by Keith Field.

Typeset by Jean Cussons Typesetting, Diss, Norfolk

Printed and bound in India by Replika Press Pvt Ltd

CONTENTS

LIST OF DIAGRAMS

FOREWORD

By the Duke of Devonshire, Chatsworth

I am delighted to write a foreword to this remarkable book by Nij Vyas. Sheepdog trialling is very much part of the culture of the Peak District, where I am lucky enough to live. Trials were started with the simple object of testing one shepherd's skill with his dog against another. Longshaw Sheepdog Trials, of which I have had the honour of being President twice in my life, is the oldest established sheepdog trials in England, having now been run for the last 111 years.

To witness the competitors on the beautiful open landscape above the Hope Valley is an experience that all true lovers of the countryside should experience at least once. It is enthralling and fascinating, and it has a crucial practical application: good sheepdogs save a shepherd a vast amount of walking, and enable him to look after his flock. For the relationship between dog and handler to be successful, an enormous amount of dedicated practice is required.

Nij Vyas was not born into farming, but as you will discover from this book he has become an experienced and successful sheepdog handler. His commitment is even greater than most as he has to travel twenty miles to work and train his dogs every day, and in this case every day means just that, every single day.

This book is not just an account of one man's love affair with sheepdogs and sheepdog trials. The author has many fascinating and some-times provocative new ideas. His aim is to give hope to newcomers, but also to help people who are already experienced in the sport. He has many tips to overcome the difficulties that all of those who participate will have met.

I can commend this book with great enthusiasm for anyone who is the slightest bit interested in sheepdog trials, be it participant or spectator. There are many new ideas here, and the story of the author's involvement in the sport is fascinating: together these strands make for a compelling read.

The Duke of Devonshire, Chatsworth, Derbyshire.
(Photo copyright Earl of Burlington)

DEDICATION

Dedicated to my wife Jo for providing me with the self-belief to buy a breed of dog I once knew nothing about, to compete in a sport I also knew nothing about, and for giving me drive and impetus to follow my dreams.

The author.

ACKNOWLEDGEMENTS

There are times when either adults or children have to be forced into things they feel uncomfortable with, and in my case it was buying a Border Collie puppy. How fickle people can be! Following weeks of having to be persuaded to buy a puppy named Oliver, it took only a matter of hours for this puppy to become 'mine'. And had I not had this new pup it is highly likely that I would never have introduced myself to Gwyn Morgan. Rather than spending my weekends out and about all over the country chasing sheep, I would probably have been a disgruntled, miserable, bad-tempered, politically incorrect Education Welfare Officer, too old and too unfit to play village cricket (on second thoughts I probably am, some of the time). Being a typical Gemini, symbolized by the twins, I have led two distinctly different lives since 1992. However, no sooner do I set foot into my Hilux pickup than some dramatic transformation seems to take place, as if I were entering Narnia through the wardrobe, though without the ice queen and mythical creatures. The life I love and relate to most is that which my dogs are part of, being out in the open British countryside. I owe all this to my wife Jo for introducing me to this new life.

No one prepares you for parenthood, but goodness me: each year that Kieran and Laura have grown older, they have made me feel younger. They have shared in all my highs and lows, and above all our world is bound tightly together by humour and laughter. There is no drug better than this for lifting the soul. They are both also immensely competitive, yet gracious in defeat, which fills me with great pride. To them I owe my sanity.

My sincere thanks also to Gwyn Morgan, my dear friend, who encouraged me to work my dogs on sheep for the very first time. A friend always tells it how it is. There is no glossing over the cracks, there is honesty and respect, there is rivalry and gamesmanship but without conflict, and there is humour – and this is what I have with Gwyn.

To be successful at trials requires a good dog with character. Dogs are not born with character, it has to be developed. The generosity of three men – Bryn and Marcus Pugh, and Robert Beesley – in welcoming me with open arms and giving me the freedom to work my dogs on the Caudal Hills, is the single most important factor that has enabled me to train my dogs to a high enough standard to give me confidence to compete with the best handlers in the land. The hills have given meaning to my training, and have given the dogs that individual strength of character without which they would have remained mediocre.

For the three wise men, namely Allan Heaton, John Griffiths and Aled Owen, who have unselfishly mentored me and given advice and time, I hope that I have been a good student. If not, I dare say there is still time!

I am also very grateful to Dr Angie Untisz, Frances Gavin, Aled Owen, John Griffiths, Timothy Longton and Jim Cropper for their contributions in this book, which I am certain will be received with the greatest of enthusiasm.

A note of thanks must also go to Doug Stewart, whose idea it was for me to write this book, for helping me to realize my potential, and for giving me the self-belief to undertake this project, acting as devil's advocate, for providing

Spot and Skerry.

calm reason and rationale. I hope above all else that Doug benefits more than most from this book as he ventures out on training Skerry's daughter, Clunie, towards trials competition.

A final vote of thanks must go to all the people with whom I compete. We share a marvellous hobby and pastime, and without the Border Collie our life would have a big void in it.

On 21 October 2006 I experienced such a void, a void that has stayed with me to the present day: on this fateful day Jo broke the news to me that Skerry had been killed in a road traffic accident, running away from fireworks. I was heartbroken, and consumed with the most terrible guilt that I should have prevented this from happening. That guilt lives with me still, it travels with me wherever I go, and it creeps up on me when I least expect it and reduces me to an emotional wreck, for a split second, whilst I gather my thoughts. Then two years after her last season, Skerry's mother, Fly, once again came into season, and on an impulse born totally out of emotion I took her to be mated, not to Aled's Bob, but to Roy, a son of Bob.

Eight weeks later the first and only pup to look like Skerry was born. Of course that was the one for me. Wanting to keep the memory of Skerry alive, I chose to use the first two letters of her name and called the pup Skye. On 17 May 2009 Skye gave me by far the best run I have ever had with any dog at two years and three months of age, and won her first open trial with the last run of the trial, with probably the worst packet of sheep let out all day. As I left for home that most terrible feeling of guilt about Skerry once again hit me with a vengeance, and I found myself in tears as I left the trial field – but not all were tears of sadness. A hundred metres or so on, the guilt in my mind now had a companion: hope. Quite miraculously the guilt became far easier to live with, and gradually turned into determination, to make up the lost time. Time, as they say, is a great healer.

Finally I would like to thank the following individuals: the Duke of Devonshire (for the Foreword), John Craven OBE (for his review), Gwyn Jones (for his review), Julie Wright (for proofreading), Dr Doug Stewart (for proofreading), Maurice Gregory (for his generosity in allowing me to use land and sheep) and Paul Jackson for assistance with diagrams.

The photographs have been provided by the following:

Nij Vyas – pages 15, 16, 19, 24, 26, 28, 30 (both), 33 (both), 42, 49 (both), 58, 59, 60, 66, 69, 78, 79, 83, 89, 90, 102, 104, 107, 108, 144, 147 (bottom), 148, 150, 157, 166, 168, 172, 174 (top), 177, 187, 189, 193, 197 and 198.

Joanne Cooper – pages 8, 13, 41, 73, 94, 95, 96, 103, 112, 123 (both), 124, 126, 127, 133, 134, 136, 137, 142, 151, 158 (both), 160 and 178.

Andi Beazeley – pages 25, 50 (both), 86 (both), 87 (both), 100, 103, 106, 117 (both), 118, 139, 162, 174 (bottom), 188, 192 and 196.

William James, Target Studios – pages 2 and 10.

Mariska De Hoogt – page 98.

Joanne Vyas – pages 146, 147 (top), 152 (both) and 153.

Michael Rickett – pages 101, 109 (both) and 121.

Kim Gibson (© Kim Gibson, Nidderdale Sheepdogs) – pages 17 and 184.

Gwyn Morgan – page 99.

Tim Foster – pages 161, 164 and 180.

Bill Burlington – page 7.

Jason Senior (© Leicester Mercury Media Group Ltd) – page 191.

INTRODUCTION

I recall Glyn Jones, of Bodfari in North Wales, saying many years ago that you can kick a quad bike but a dog you can talk to. This struck a chord with me, and made me think that what all species have in common, including man, is the need for understanding and resentment to change.

The purpose of this book is to enable sheepdog handlers and enthusiasts to discover and use the many wonderful and natural attributes the Border Collie possesses for working with sheep. Even before any training takes place the collie is gifted with raw but natural abilities for speed, diligence, guile and tenacity. And being blessed with so many abilities the Border Collie must never be turned into a robot, simply waiting to be given commands: there are many situations where the collie's natural reactions will not only be correct, but quicker than any command you can deliver, and these reactions and instincts are frequently the correct ones.

I hope this book will offer an insight into what is necessary to be successful in sheepdog trials, and that it will help improve both your own and your dog's performance. It is also designed to give you a structure for your training, and a realistic expectation and self-belief of what you can achieve with your dog. In no way is it a criticism of other handlers' methods or styles of handling: rather it is based on observations of success achieved in other human and canine disciplines and sports, by other sheepdog handlers, and of course drawn from my own experience. I am full of admiration for any man, woman or child who takes the time to go out with their dog and try their hand at working with sheep, and even more so for those who are happy to impart their skills and knowledge unselfishly so that others may experience the joys of winning. Very few of us enter trials for the prize money; however, all of us work, train and compete with our collie friends for the pleasure of a job well done, punctuated with a 'That'll do' to mark our satisfaction with our dogs.

In every discipline there are 'horses for courses', and some dogs will undoubtedly have greater potential than others. However, I honestly believe that given time and understanding handlers can improve their own ability and that of their dogs, and at least fulfil their potential. By recognizing your own failings you will be better placed to maximize your dog's potential. If you do not, or cannot, accept that *you* are at fault, then you may well conclude that your dog's poor performance is because *the dog* is being inept. In some cases this can result in the dog being rehomed, and in many cases handlers can become angry, frustrated and disillusioned with trialling. You only have to look at the large number of cases where dogs have failed to fulfil their potential and have been sold, then subsequently have gone on to achieve success with their new handlers. This newfound success can only be due to a change in the training regime, or because the dog is allowed a bit more time in which to mature. Of course some dogs will suit some handlers more than others, and this is why the process of selecting the right puppy or dog to match and compliment your handling style is so important.

At every trial there are just six places for the winning dogs. This book will hopefully lead to more people challenging for those places, thereby raising the level of competition; in turn this will improve the standard at which Border Collies work. If more people can go home feeling that their dogs have worked to their potential, then my aim will have been achieved. Because trialling relies on an element of luck, it can be a great leveller, and I hope that by trying to improve the standard of handling and training, the hobby triallist will play a more significant part and be able to hold their own against farmers and shepherds. But whichever group of handlers you belong to, we all have one thing in common, and that is the tools we work with, namely the Border Collie. And a good worker never blames his tools.

Apart from the dog, the other major factors that come into play are the opportunity to work with large numbers of sheep on a frequent basis, and the type of terrain available. There is no doubt in my mind that those with access to hill or mountain terrain or moorland to practise their daily shepherding tasks will always have an advantage over those with smaller flat fields, as the former offers a greater opportunity for the dog to rely on and practise inbred instincts. We all have hidden strengths, but we can only ever realize them when we are put in a situation that

tests us to the limit. On hill terrain, greater decision making on the part of the dog is called for. Many dogs resist aspects of training if they cannot see the reason for having to work in a particular way, whether it is a wide flank or to work at a greater distance from the sheep, at a particular pace. For example, dogs that work the hill learn very quickly, and in a quite uncontrived manner, that they need to run wide to cover the whole flock, as there may be dips and hollows where sheep could be hidden from view. It is the nature of the terrain itself that makes the dog realize why he needs to run wide.

Dogs will also become far more at ease with having to run blind or unsighted from the sheep, often using their sense of smell to find them. If in everyday work all a dog has to do to locate its sheep is to look a short distance in front, its sense of smell will be less developed and fine tuned than that of a dog which has to find its sheep over difficult terrain. Although all dogs are gifted with a keen sense of smell they nevertheless need to be able to practise using their nose, and to develop confidence in their ability to use it. The very nature of hills and mountains

Peak Forest looking out on to Eldon Hill.

obliges the dogs to rely on their other senses, rather than sight alone.

My own dog Jade, who suffered from CEA (collie eye anomaly, *see* p. 22) and was partially blind in both eyes, came to rely almost totally on sense of smell when she was old and when the light faded in the evening. Whilst out on walks she would wander off, as old dogs do, yet she would unerringly return to the car on her own by using her nose.

Not everyone is lucky enough to have a hill or a mountain in their near vicinity, but one thing I am sure of, and that is that just as our children go to university to further their education, to be successful in sheepdog trials both you and your dogs must be taken out of your comfort zone if you are going to graduate and find your hidden strengths. To achieve success you must be prepared to go the extra mile, to study your dogs and your techniques, to look at both the faults and what you do well. The advent of the video camera in particular has provided the means for handlers to improve their skills and to learn from their mistakes, to analyse and assess the finer points of technique from the comfort of their living room. The availability of DVDs of international and world sheepdog trials is also a great resource and a means to learn and progress, to watch top handlers and glean knowledge from them. It may seem an obvious thing to say, but should you need advice, ask someone for it. And if you want something desperately enough, then you must be prepared to work hard for it.

I, like many others, cannot afford, nor do I have the inclination to buy or indeed keep lots of dogs, and therefore believe that you have to make the most of what you have got. Also many people are not comfortable with selling dogs. I hope that this book gives hope if things are not going quite to plan. Bearing in mind that most of us spend more time with our dogs than our partners, dogs, like marriages, need to be worked on over a long period of time. There will be good times, there will be some bad times,

there may even be some sad times, but if you persevere the memories will indeed be special. It is a privilege to share my life with my collie friends, and I strive to do my best by them, as they do for me.

There are four names that feature regularly in the prize lists: John Ryan Griffiths (Talysarn), Tim Longton (Quernmore), Aled Owen (Ty Nant) and Jim Cropper (Bacup). Their handling of dogs is the envy of many people and each of them has described, in this book, in their own words, what it is that makes them successful handlers, what they look for when selecting a dog, and whether luck has played any part in their success.

Whether you choose to breed and train your own pup or to buy one which is ready trained, your journey will be an exciting one, with many highs and lows. The rest of this book will take you through the journey from being a young hopeful prospect to a useful trials dog. It will provide you with the means to resolve some major health, training and behaviour issues, as well as prepare you for becoming a successful and competent sheepdog trainer for trials or simply farm work, using methods and theories that are innovative and modern. We are living in times when the countryside and country sports are under close scrutiny. The welfare of sheep and sheepdogs is paramount, and it is my intention that handlers will learn to adopt a caring and empathetic, yet highly effective training regime.

BLENDING THE OLD WITH THE NEW

Old-fashioned methods of training dogs invariably involved a combination of force, reward and punishment. Handlers were heavy handed and relied on force rather than subtlety and psychology to effect change. The 1990s, however, brought about a new emphasis, that of training with kinder, gentler methods, using

Guiding Principle

'Power is of two kinds. One is obtained by the fear of punishment, and the other by acts of love. Power based on love is a thousand times more effective and permanent than the one derived from fear of punishment.'   Mahatma Gandhi

food to shape behaviour, rewarding positive behaviour and ignoring bad behaviour. Karen Pryor's book *Don't Shoot the Dog – The New Art of Teaching and Training Dogs* had a profound influence on me, as not only did it discuss changing the behaviour of dogs and other animals, such as dolphins, but also that of humans. Teaching dogs to stand, lie down and so on became more enjoyable; results were quickly attained, and the dogs seemed happy to work for rewards. Using these methods to teach the basics became the norm for me, prior to taking dogs to sheep, particularly because dogs

as young as six to seven weeks old responded well to this form of training.

The term 'sheepdog trial' suggests that working with both sheep and dogs can be a testing time. This is indeed true; however, the term does conveniently leave out 'man' from the equation. The real trial is when the handler is asked to participate in it too, and work with two different species, each with a mistrust of one another and subjecting them to unnatural and gruelling demands. Both sheep and dogs have a naturally intrinsic mistrust of their human counterpart, having no idea, concept or inclination of what consequences will ensue. To earn the trust of two different species without losing faith and respect, and without inducing fear and trepidation, is truly the biggest trial of all. For me, to achieve this with no experience of sheep and no mentor to guide me, became the ultimate challenge, with only my experience as a dog trainer to fall back on.

My wife Jo and I become dog trainers in 1988 and I started our own club, Bertie Dog Training, in 1991. I have worked with a large variety of dog breeds, dealing with issues

Honest we mean you no harm!

Gwyn Morgan, my friend and confidant.

involving basic pet obedience to quite severe behavioural problems such as sheep worrying and killing, with dogs suffering from separation anxiety to those which have been maltreated, and aggressive dogs. I also train farmers and Border Collie enthusiasts to work sheep either for trials or to help in their daily work.

Through a series of chance meetings with people from both breed shows as well as trialling, my interest in the Border Collie was further intensified by one man: Gwyn Morgan. Gwyn farms in the midst of Snowdonia, near Caernarfon. His farm stands a mile or so off the beaten track at the top of a hill, surrounded on the south side by an ancient forest overlooking the Snowdon Mountains. Having farmed some 120 acres, of which 80 acres is grassland and 40 acres forest, Gwyn keeps sheep, cattle, poultry and horses. He has since scaled down so that he can enjoy and spend more time training and working his dogs. His influence over my life and subsequent trialling career has been immense, and as was the case when we first met in 1987, he remains my adviser, my confi-

dant and my dear friend. North Wales is where the journey started; where it ends remains to be seen.

Having been encouraged to work my dogs I then took it a step further, competing in my first trial in 1992 at Pontllyfni, North Wales. Being a novice not only to sheepdog trialling but also working with sheep, I generally found advice very difficult to come by, though this was with the exception of that offered by Allan Heaton (Brandsby, York), John Griffiths (Talysarn, North Wales) and later, Aled Owen (Ty Nant, Corwen). I was generally met with either one-word answers or simply told to 'watch the top handlers'. This was good advice; however, I needed a lot more: I needed to know what I was supposed to be looking out for, and why. In many cases the genius of the top men was not always evident at trials, apart from their success, but rather it was the manner in which they trained their dogs that the true genius could be observed. I recall ringing Allan Heaton in 1992 for his opinion on Aled Owen's Ben (129820), as I was thinking of using him at stud. Allan's response was 'Ben is a great dog, but I don't know how much of that is due to Aled as he is a great trainer and handler'! (Quote courtesy Allan and Mary Heaton.)

As a rule I found the top handlers' dogs worked very well; however, what I needed to know was what aspects of their training made them perform to such a high standard. I was once given the following advice by a friend: 'If you look at something long enough or often enough you will discover something new that you haven't noticed before.' I have found this advice to be true time and time again. I found myself watching handlers, and slowly but surely the picture started to unfold. I began to break down what they were doing into the smallest parts, constantly asking myself why they did things in a particular way, and more importantly to be able to put a label to it. For example:

- Why did they not ask the dog to lie down at the end of an outrun?
- Why did they take so long to open the pen gate?
- Why did they keep the sheep moving towards the pen?
- Why did they take so long in the shedding ring rather than make an opportunity?
- Why did they move purposefully into the shedding ring?

Mr Jim Easton presents the Wilkinson Sword to Allan and Mary Heaton.

Ask ten farmers how and at what age they train their dogs, and each one will probably give a different answer based on their own experience and how they were taught and what they found to be successful. I managed to untangle all the information I had acquired, and slowly but surely began to make sense of what the handlers were doing – and what was more important, why. Then began the experiment of putting into practice what I had learned. With each young puppy I reared I tried something different until finally I was happy with how my dogs were turning out. I remain cautious,

however, and constantly remind myself that the quest for knowledge is a never-ending process, and am excited by learning new ways to manage age-old, traditional shepherding tasks.

Above all I make it a priority that my dogs work willingly and with enthusiasm, based on mutual respect between dog and handler. Hopefully this book will go some way to sharing with its readers the finer points that I was able to discover on my journey, which started on the greens of a cricket field when I was eleven years old, and progressed to when I took up sheepdog trialling in 1992, culminating in representing England at the Kelso International Sheepdog Trials in 2006 with Skerry.

CHAPTER 1

WHETHER TO BUY OR BREED YOUR OWN DOGS

TAKING CONTROL OF THE BREEDING PROGRAMME

There are of course advantages and disadvantages to both breeding and buying in dogs. Ultimately which path you follow will be determined by your views, your personal preference and circumstances.

Ever since I can remember, my life has followed a similar pattern, that of listening to the voice in my head, despite the anomalies it throws. At least then I could either take the blame for my resulting actions, or indeed the credit. Most of all, however, doing things in my own way gave me a tremendous opportunity for learning and developing my own concepts about training and breeding.

Monitoring Seasons

A bitch will normally have her first season when she is about eight to ten months old (sometimes later), and then will have one on average every six months. However, in my experience the science has never been so exact, and I have found that working bitches, like modern-day women, want to concentrate on building a career first before settling down to family life. For the past twenty years I have found it to be the norm that if the bitch is working, her first season is actually delayed, with the first at about twelve to fifteen months, and subsequent

seasons following at around eight to fifteen months.

Due to the irregular nature of my bitches' seasons I found it useful to chart their occurrence on the computer: I would note the date of the season, and over time would be able to project when their following seasons might occur, based on their historical sequence. I also kept details of the bitch's associated behaviour. After a period of four or five years it became apparent that each female followed a certain pattern. Lara, for example, always came into season every eight or nine months. Two months prior to her season her moods would fluctuate and she would become aggressive and intolerant of other bitches in the pack. She also lacked concentration at trials during this period. When she finally came into season it was not unusual for her to go off her food for a short while. She was always ready for mating on the ninth day of her season, and would be mated for a second time on the eleventh day.

Fly came into season for the first time at nine months but with a false season – there was no bleeding, but the dogs were very interested. Six months later she came into season properly. Her second season then followed eight months after the start of the first season, but she would not stand for mating until the sixteenth day. Her third season was exactly six months later, and on this occasion three months before she came on heat she developed aggressive behaviour,

Skerry nursing her one and only litter.

she also lost concentration whilst working, and suffered a loss of appetite. After five years of age her seasons were between fifteen months and two years apart, also her seasons seemed to last considerably longer and she stood for mating far later than was normal for Border Collies. Once her season was finished it was not unusual for her to repeat the cycle only a few days later. Fly was mated to Aled Owen's Bob in April 2000, but this mating revealed no pups when she was scanned. She then came back into season four weeks later and was mated again. This time it was successful, and she had a litter of seven pups, of which I kept Spot (251155) and Skerry (251154)

Skerry inherited her mother's seasonal behaviour and took it a stage further. On average her seasons were around fifteen months apart, and her last two seasons were each four to five weeks long; they also consisted of two cycles, with only the second one being fertile. She was only bred from once, and this mating took place over her two cycles; she produced six pups sixty-one days after the last mating. Just to be totally safe she was mated on six occasions – I

didn't pay much attention to science on that occasion!

Had I not kept records on Skerry and Fly, it is unlikely that I could have timed the mating correctly and had any puppies from either of them.

How Many Litters?

I have always believed that breeding should be a matter of quality and not quantity, and have only ever bred from a bitch when I wanted a pup for myself; financial gain has been furthest from my thoughts. I have also, on more than one occasion, had to put up with problems that were not of my own making, which has been a bitter pill to swallow: in terms of dog breeding I like to be in control of my own destiny, and have always been more tolerant of mistakes that I have made, as opposed to living with the consequences of other people's mistakes. This is not to say that my policy is infallible, but simply pointing out that in any walk of life people always cope better if they own up to their mistakes.

I am not an advocate of breeding from a bitch at her every season, or even every other season. Having only ever kept a small number of dogs I have always preferred to have my bitches competing and working, rather than nursing countless litters of puppies.

To my mind puppies receive their first and most crucial lessons from their mother, and this is from the moment they are born. Furthermore their strength of character is closely associated to the time, effort and bonding that takes place from birth to six or seven weeks, both between littermates and with their mother. A good breeder should allow for the puppies' education to be as natural as possible, and should trust their mother to provide guidance at the different stages of growth. Between the ages of four to twelve weeks is a critical period of development for the puppies, and it makes sense that the time and experience they share with mum – feeding, being groomed, being stimulated through licking, the rough and tumble of play, and being disciplined – lays the foundations for a stable and balanced upbringing. This is when they learn about dominance, and become armed with the strategies that will help them cope with different situations for the whole of their lifetime.

It also makes sense to conclude that if the brood bitch is a stable, well balanced and well socialized type, she will be a positive role model for her puppies. If, on the other hand, a brood bitch has been extensively bred from, it is understandable that she will not relish the caring and nurturing role, and her puppies' education will be greatly compromised. Furthermore she will resent any attention from the puppies during feeding and playtime.

There have been many occasions at my dog club where I have observed puppies as young as seven or eight weeks looking lifeless, and petrified of life in general – and this includes their owners. In some cases this was due to poor socialization, but in the majority of cases we identified that these pups had been separated from their mother either at birth or at around five weeks, or they were bred on puppy farms. Even one extra week in the life of a puppy spent with its mother and littermates can have tremendous benefits, as long as the experience is a positive one.

Some puppies were not only frightened, but screamed when their owners touched them or picked them up; some even growled and were aggressive, and looked thoroughly traumatized. They had evidently failed to thrive either amongst their littermates, or since leaving the litter and moving in with their new families, and sometimes their antisocial behaviour was reinforced by their owners, who felt terribly sorry for them. Many of these pups were too inhibited to play, or chase around, or tug at toys, but would hide under a chair with a look of resignation, quivering and shaking in anticipation of any new experience.

With regard to breeding etiquette, I have always tried to observe the following principles:

- Not to breed from a bitch until she is about two years of age, at the earliest, coinciding with her second season.
- To limit the number of litters produced by any one bitch to four in her lifetime at most, although the average has been about three.
- Not to breed from a bitch after the age of eight.

The only time I have deviated from the above points was when tragically I lost Skerry in 2006. I was desperate to replace her for the forthcoming summer season, but just couldn't find the right dog to buy. Then amazingly, after a two-year break, Fly finally came into season – but she was just over nine years old, so I was in a dilemma: in my book she was too old to breed from, yet she was in peak fitness and still working hard, and had produced only two litters to date. Finally I decided to have her checked over by a vet, who gave her a clear bill of health. She produced a litter of five puppies with no problems, and was the model mum in raising her litter. I kept a pretty young bitch called Skye.

Why I Prefer to Breed my own Pups

It is very rare for me to consider buying a puppy because I prefer to have control not only over how the puppies are raised, but also how the pregnancy is managed. The care of the brood bitch is crucial, and careful management of her nutritional and health needs during pregnancy and lactation can have a profound effect on how the pups develop both physically and neurologically.

I also believe in having my bitches scanned, normally on two occasions, between four and five weeks after mating and around eight weeks after mating, just before the pups are born. Some people do not believe in scanning, but I have found it invaluable, not only so that I know how many puppies to expect, but also whether they have a healthy heartbeat or not. Also by the time the bitch is scanned for a second time the pups are ready to be born and it is possible to see if they are facing the right way, or if they are breeched, where the rump is presented first with the hind legs tucked under the body. Furthermore, if you know how many puppies your bitch is expecting you can increase the diet accordingly, thereby ensuring that their nervous system is not starved, which could lead to later complications and subsequent behavioural problems. Information regarding problems during pregnancy and during birth can be invaluable in predicting and coping with future problems.

In 2009 Gwyn Morgan's bitch Gwen produced twelve pups. As Gwyn had not had the bitch scanned, each pup after the seventh born was a surprise to him. After the ninth pup

---

Tip

Remember that during pregnancy bitches require increased amounts of food: this can be up to a 50 per cent increase in their normal daily amount, and during lactation up to a 90 per cent increase in the third week. The amounts depend on the size of the litter, and should be increased and decreased gradually.

Gwen took a breather, and Gwyn assumed that she had finished giving birth and took her for a short walk. On her return Gwen then produced three more pups. You can imagine the relief Gwyn must have felt that Gwen had produced each pup without the need for veterinary assistance. Had there been complications Gwyn would have been very much in the dark and not been forearmed to help Gwen. (Information courtesy of Gwyn Morgan.)

The main reason I like to breed my own puppies is because I can influence their education right from the start, and can observe them when they are feeding and starting to develop play behaviour. Almost from the very onset you might observe that the same puppies nearly always take up a position at the rear teats, where the milk is usually more plentiful. This not only shows strength of character but also decision making, and by keeping notes at the different stages of growth you may notice a pattern between a puppy that suckles from a rear teat, and subsequent behaviour traits as mentioned above.

Another aspect of training you can achieve early is to introduce a recall whistle every time you bring food to the puppies. As puppies are fed many times a day they will become easily conditioned to a recall whistle. Many of the puppies that I have bred and subsequently sold to new owners will react positively to my recall whistle, even as adults, despite my not having played a hand in their upbringing.

Early socialization is absolutely crucial to the development of a dog's character, and given that between four to twelve weeks is a critical period in the puppies' development, the breeder is best placed, apart from the mother, to educate them. This can include exposing them to the following situations and experiences:

- Frequent car journeys from as early as four weeks so they become accustomed to motion.
- Contact with children and adults, and learning to be frequently handled.
- Contact with pets such as rabbits and guinea pigs, ducks, hens and so on.
- Mental stimulation by offering them toys, and obstacles to overcome such as steps, or placing a big box with a hole cut in it so they learn to find their way out. In this way puppies are obliged to develop 'coping' strategies.
- At four weeks old I place the puppies in an outdoor kennel, giving them the opportunity to experience different weather conditions and various outdoor stimuli.
- Controlling feeding regimes can either make them keen eaters and, therefore, highly motivated by food, or lazy eaters that are less greedy (*see* Chapter 4, The Passive Resistance Theory).

Hereditary Defects

When breeding, it is easy only to consider the working traits of the parents, for example their outrun, power, natural pace and so forth. However, it is just as crucial to take into account the dog's genetic makeup and any hereditary defects and abnormalities as well as conformation. Although progress has been very slow, many farmers and trials competitors have now started to embrace sensible breeding practices, such as DNA testing for congenital eye defects, testing for hearing (the BAER test – brainstem auditory evoked response), hip dysplasia and so on. These good practices are crucial to the survival of what I consider to be the finest dog breed of all, so that nowadays it is quite rare to find quality collies being advertised by the roadside at £50 – although there are instances of this still happening.

The three main areas currently causing debate concerning the Border Collie are collie eye anomaly (CEA), centralized progressive retinal atrophy (PRA) and trapped neutrophil syndrome (TNS): these are discussed below.

Collie Eye Anomaly (CEA)

I have always ensured that my Border Collies are tested for CEA, optimally when they are between five and six weeks of age, either by the breeder or by me, as recommended by the British Veterinary Association (BVA). And when a breeder did not routinely have a litter screened, it was not unusual for me to pay for the whole litter to be eye tested, prior to buying a puppy, thereby giving me the peace of mind that I would have sound breeding stock. In its simplest form CEA causes tiny holes in the retina, resulting in partial blindness in mild cases, and in the worst scenario, total detachment of the retina, though this is extremely rare. CEA is produced by a recessive gene, so for a dog to be affected both parents would have to be carriers or affected. The limitation of the BVA scheme is that it only determines dogs that are actually affected: it does not identify carriers.

Breeding from affected or carrying stock has always been discouraged, both by the International Sheepdog Society and the Border Collie Club of Great Britain. Nowadays DNA (deoxyribonucleic acid) testing, in the form of either blood or swab tests, has made it possible to determine whether dogs are normal, carriers

Expected Results of Breeding Strategies for Inherited Recessive Diseases (*see* References, 'Outcomes of breeding') (Courtesy Susan Pearce-Kelling, OptiGen, LLC, copyright holder.)

Parent 1 Genotype	Parent 2 Genotype 1		
	Normal	Carrier	Affected
Normal	All = Normal	1/2 = Normal 1/2 = Carriers	All = Carriers
Carrier	1/2 = Normal 1/2 = Carriers	1/4 = Normal 1/2 = Carriers 1/4 = Affected	1/2 = Carriers 1/2 = Affected
Affected	All = Carriers	1/2 = Carriers 1/2 = Affected	All = Affected

or affected. The cost implication of DNA testing is, of course, greater; however, this is offset by the fact that where two genetically 'normal' dogs are bred from, the resulting pups will also be 'normal' and will not require testing. As a result, breeders are able to charge a higher price when selling 'genetically normal' puppies.

Centralized Progressive Retinal Atrophy (PRA) (see References)

The BVA recommend that dogs are checked regularly for CPRA, which has been observed in dogs of between eighteen months and nine years of age. As yet there is no genetic test available for CPRA. Peripheral vision is retained for a long time. Generally, vision is better in low light, and better for moving or distant objects. Not all affected dogs go blind. Secondary cataracts are also common.

Trapped Neutrophil Syndrome (TNS) (See References)

TNS is an autosomal recessive condition that affects the immune system. Neutrophils are required to protect the body from infection, and symptoms are quite varied, with some pups born looking normal, whilst others are rather small, with fine bones and a small head, traits that become more obvious at around sixteen weeks of age. One of the first indications of TNS is a bad reaction to vaccination, when the pup will show signs of fever.

Frazer Allen and Boyd Jones were the first to describe TNS and its related symptoms, in 1996; until that time Border Collie owners were all but ignorant of the condition. Indeed many people in farming circles and on the sheepdog trials scene are still unaware of what TNS is. Although blood tests can be used to determine low levels of neutrophils, TNS can now be diagnosed by DNA testing at the University of New South Wales, Australia.

Ongoing Health and Conformation Issues

In recent years two other conditions, namely ceroid lipofuscinosis (CL), or storage disease, and glaucoma have also become associated with the Border Collie. Reported incidences of these conditions have been rare, however, and research in these areas is ongoing.

Mac shows perfect poise and guile.

The Border Collie Breed Council is to be congratulated for leading from the front in providing the facility and funding for research and testing on health matters, and for providing up-to-date information on current and ongoing health issues.

Sometimes a certain trait may not constitute a defect as such, but nevertheless is an important determining feature. For example, the size of a dog is often significant, as is the type of bone structure it has: thus a strongly built, tall dog with heavy bone can tire easily and lack in stamina, particularly if it is the type of dog that gives 150 per cent effort all the time, rather than working in a quieter, more conservative manner. Nevertheless, a number of farmers who graze their sheep on the Welsh mountains prefer this type of dog: big, strong and well boned. Often the answer lies in particular breeding lines, in that in some the propensity is to be able to work all day, whilst in others the dog will tire more easily and suffer in a hot climate, particularly if it has a rough coat. Of course, stamina also depends on the amount of work that a dog does, combined with its age and experience. On their own many of these characteristics may not be particularly significant; however, when combined the results can be extremely influential.

Like many others, I tend to place greater significance on the dogs in the first four genera-tions of a pedigree, because these dogs are accessible to us, or we can relate to many of them. In many cases we have seen or heard of them, or know of people who have knowledge of, and information about them. However, it never ceases to amaze me that whenever I breed a litter of pups, with great regularity one of them appears to be a throwback to maybe the sixth and seventh generation. This is a good reminder that you can try and follow a set pathway, but nothing is ever written in stone!

Line Breeding or Outcross?

When breeding your own dogs it is important always to bear in mind that all dogs and lines have their particular faults, and a good breeder will always aim to breed out the faults and focus on improving the strengths. Of course, what one person considers a fault, another may class as a strength, depending on their level of experience and particular farming needs. Furthermore, some people may want what is commonly known as a 'Saturday afternoon dog' as they do not have enough work for their dogs, whereas others need a strong dog that can move a flock of 400 ewes with ease. The breeders of Border Collies carry a huge responsibility as to how the breed evolves, and to ensure its continuity as the world's premier herding dog.

I have heard many discussions over the years at both trials and breed shows, and have been worried by a change in ideals in both disciplines. It is indeed quite true that there are fewer shepherds now than thirty or forty years ago, and the large sheep producers of yesteryear are few and far between. Average flock sizes are now greatly reduced, and farmers are tending towards having a softer, weaker type of dog that is equally at home on the farm as a trial field. But is this really the way to go? Once the qualities that make a truly strong farm dog have been lost they will take decades to restore back into the breed.

In trialling we have been, and are truly blessed with some great handlers who have experience of driving flocks in their thousands on horseback with eight dogs or more working in unison and under control, over mountainous terrain. Each year the International Sheepdog Trials set out to provide a test for dogs which simulates these conditions. However, I would like to see more open trials that test the dogs to this standard, and which incorporate double gather elements (occasionally), shed and singling. Furthermore, trials should reflect and enhance the strengths of a Border Collie. For example, the fetch element in a trial should require minimal commands: if a dog cannot bring sheep to the handler and balance them without minimal commands, then this reflects a flaw either in the dog or the handler's training methods.

I have always preferred to stick to lines that I am familiar with, purely because I have grown to understand them and to cope with certain faults. But even with successful bitches, when selecting for breeding I try to be honest with myself about them, and make a list of their faults and the frustrations I have experienced with certain aspects of their work. I then look for stud dogs that do not have these faults, as well as characteristics and aspects of their working style that I admire. I prefer to find dogs that can compliment my bitches, rather than choosing dogs that are successful and winning frequently. Furthermore, if I find a dog that has all the characteristics I am looking for, then often I will use the father of that dog as well as consider the maternal side of the pedigree.

There has always been great confusion between the terms 'inbreeding' and 'line breeding'. Many breeders believe that if the percentage of breeding is greater or equal to 50 per cent, this is classed as inbreeding: however, there is confusion even between geneticists, and some do not adhere to this theory. The following pedigree shows the level of inbreeding:

Spot – never a Saturday afternoon dog.

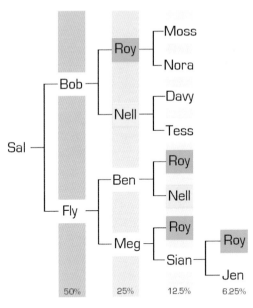

| 50% | 25% | 12.5% | 6.25% |

Mock inbreeding pedigree.

Roy has 25% + 12½% + 12½% + 6¼% = 56¼%

Nell has 25 + 12½% = 37½%

The above pedigree shows, in mathematical terms, that there is line breeding to Nell 37½ per cent and inbreeding to Roy 56¼ per cent. Ultimately it is the virtues or shortcomings of both dogs that are of greatest importance.

Puppy Selection

The first dog I ever bought was a red merle Border Collie by the name of Oliver, named after Oliver Hardy. We went to a farmer in Church Greasley, in Derbyshire; he opened the door to an outbuilding, and several strangely coloured pups ran out in every direction. One pup stood out as bolder and noticeably independent from the others; he was differently marked and outgoing in character (some would argue that the pup was my mirror image). Without hesitation I chose him and called him Oliver. He πgrew into the most stunningly handsome and outstanding dog: he had presence, he was strong and fearless, and he was far too good for a novice handler. I don't mind admitting he was wasted on me. He worked sheep and

Oliver – my first Border Collie, a red merle bred back to Bosworth Coon.

cattle equally well and took his commands, except the stop, the very instant they were delivered. What I would give now for a dog of his character!

Talking to farmers I have come across a variety of methods of puppy selection – as well as a lot of old wives' tales. One Welsh farmer told me that his father would only pick a pup with a dark palette, another that a mottled puppy was the one for him.

Floppy ears are considered to attract ear mites and difficult to keep clean, and a prick-eared pup is preferred. Some farmers won't touch a puppy that eats grass; some leave selection to chance, and keep the last one left unsold out of a litter; others trust in their wives (good for your marriage)! Many keep the boldest or most confident pup. A wall-eyed dog is often quite popular – and so on. These days half white-faced dogs are all the rage.

Having listened to the various theories, I remained unconvinced that these were the best methods for selecting a puppy that would be successful at trials. Then in the late 1990s I came across a sheepdog training video and booklet produced by Bruce Englefield, which examined puppy selection in a more systematic way. It placed less emphasis on luck, and more on set criteria required for successful working dogs as well as good household pets. The selection method was based on tests conducted by Clarence Pfaffenberger, whose book *The New Knowledge of Dog Behaviour*, first published in 1963, offered a way for dog owners and, more importantly, breeders to predict their pup's adult temperament. Although the test would not measure the extent to which genetics determines a pup's temperament, due to environmental factors such as the nursing bitch's behaviour towards her pups from birth, it was nevertheless a good tool in helping to predict the future behaviour of dogs.

Following on from Pfaffenberger's work and from similar testing not just on puppies, but based on studies of children's development and learning stages, Wendy Volhard developed perhaps the best known test, known as the Volhard test, or PAT (puppy aptitude tests). Wendy recommends testing pups at forty-nine days of age, as this is when they are neurologically complete and when learning begins. The Volhard test is simple to administer, and tests ten elements, with each scored out of six (*see* References). The aim of the test was to match the right puppy for each handler, given their own style of handling and preferences for the dog. The tests were as follows:

1. Social attraction to people – testing confidence and dependence.
2. Following – willingness to follow a person.
3. Restraint – degree of dominance or submission combined with ease of handling.
4. Social dominance – degree of acceptance of social or physical dominance.
5. Elevation – degree of acceptance of dominance whilst having no control, for example being examined by a veterinarian.
6. Retrieving – degree of willingness to work with a human.
7. Touch sensitivity – degree of tolerance and sensitivity to touch.
8. Sound sensitivity – sensitivity to loud noises such as thunderstorms or fireworks.
9. Sight sensitivity – chase instinct or response to moving objects such as bicycles, livestock.
10. Stability – degree of startle response to a strange object.

(Courtesy Jack and Wendy Volhard, copyright holders)

The first time I used the Volhard PAT test was in the year 2000 when I bred from my own Fly, and used Aled Owen's World and International Supreme Champion Bob. I kept two pups from the litter: Spot and Skerry, both of whom went on to a successful trials career. Both scored mainly twos and threes (and of course there was an element of liking these pups, too). The attributes are shown below. The major difference between the two was their response to the sight sensitivity test; also Spot had a greater tendency to grip than Skerry. This was certainly borne out as they grew older, as Skerry settled into her work almost straightaway, once she was trained, whereas Spot was nearly four and a half before he began to settle. Spot was the more forceful and more positive (not always an advantage), whereas Skerry was kind to her sheep, which made her a lucky dog.

The Volhard interpretation of the high to mid-range scores is as follows:

Dogs achieving mostly twos:

- Like to have leadership aspirations.
- Will be hard to manage, and have the capacity to bite.
- Have lots of self-confidence.
- Should not be placed into an inexperienced home.

- Will be too unruly to be good with children and elderly people, or other animals.

Dogs achieving mostly threes:

- Are good with people and other animals, but can be difficult to live with.
- Need training, do very well at it, and learn quickly.
- Great dogs for the second-time owner.

(Courtesy Jack and Wendy Volhard, copyright holders.)

My reason for selecting dogs with scores of mainly two and three was based on Clarence Pfaffenberger's recommendations. Where more than one dog scored the same I invariably kept the dog that I liked the most in terms of character and classical markings. Of my current dogs, both Skye and Mac scored mainly twos and threes, with one marked difference: Skye scored a two/three on sight sensitivity, while Mac scored a one. Skye also scored better at the retrieve test. The interpretations of these scores for sight-sensitive dogs are as follows:

Skye, my precocious young dog, uses her nose to find sheep.

- A score of one indicates that the puppy looks, attacks and bites.
- A score of two indicates that the puppy looks, then barks with its tail held up.

The differences between Mac and Skye as adults, shown in the table below, make interesting reading:

Work elements	Mac aged three years	Skye aged two years
Outrun	Good on both sides but difficult to redirect. Stubborn	Good on both sides, easy to redirect
Lift	Naturally strong – needs holding back	Easy on sheep, very kind. Can stop short on left outrun if sheep still, and eye
Natural pace	Good pace but needs watching, head comes up	Good natural pace and holds top line beautifully
Pen	Good	Good
Shed	Good but prefers to head sheep, can see red on single (shed)	Good
Flanks	Taught to wide flank, can cut in	Naturally wide flanking but can stick due to tiny bit of eye
Gripper	Not any more – is self-assured	Has potential to grip with rams or difficult ewes
Positive	100 per cent	90 per cent
Lucky	Will be with age	Extremely
Confident	Yes, but can have uncertain moments during shed if near another packet of sheep	Yes, but can hang back on heavier sheep. Will improve with age
Flock work	Prefers flock, is quietly assertive	Not as good as Mac but will get a job done
Sensitive	10 per cent	5 per cent
Driving	Good	Good
Temperament	Good, but very work oriented; this will lessen with age	Excellent, loves people, dogs and children
Easily conditioned	Is obsessive, compulsive and cannot switch off easily from work	Easy to mould and a quick learner. Less intense
My favourite strengths	Is self-assured and can move anything	Is nimble-footed and tames sheep

LEFT: Mac – out of my Skerry and Michael Longton's Moss.

BELOW: Happy at work – Skye.

Both dogs were initially quite difficult to break, with both running through the sheep and scattering them to all corners. However, Skye learned a lot more quickly and was less of a liability than Mac. Mac caused sheep to split by placing too much pressure on them, and couldn't cope with ewes on their own: he became predatory, and in his anxiety to put the matter right, caused more problems. Also after work if he was not immediately placed on a lead he would take the opportunity to run back to the sheep even when they were out of sight a long distance from us.

Since the year 2000 when I first used the Volhard test I feel that I have been lucky with the dogs I have chosen. This might have been coincidence, or it might have been attributable to the test: only time will tell us the true impact of selecting puppies in such a way. If you have been one of the lucky ones that have represented your country regularly or won the bigger trials, then perhaps you already have the right system for you – although I would also like to know how many dogs have been discarded in the process.

If, on the other hand, your kennel is full of dogs that are 'neither useful nor ornament' because you have selected them on the basis of what they look like, or gut instinct, then you should think hard: why follow a path you know has not been fruitful in the past? You can do no worse than by trying something different. It is far better to pick a dog that suits your handling style and temperament, unless you have the knowledge and willingness to change your style of working with dogs.

I have heard it said many times that 'You are lucky to have one really good dog in your life-time' – but why is it that certain handlers always seem to be lucky, and always turn out good dogs? Are they lucky, gifted or talented?

As far as I can see, the strength of the Volhard test comes from the fact that it matches the right type of handler to the right puppy. I have spoken to and heard many stories of handlers who sold pups that did not work for them or suit them, only to discover several months down the line that those very same dogs were achieving success with their new partners. Now imagine that you were able to pick the right dog from your litter, and following months of training you achieved all you dreamed of: wouldn't that be just the perfect outcome for you and your dog?

Although many farmers and breeders do not consciously follow any set selection criteria or procedures such as the PAT test, they neverthe-less do look for similar traits as described in the tests, and this manner of selection can be just as effective as any formal testing.

BUYING AN ADULT DOG OR PUPPY

This can be a chancy affair. A pedigree is only worth the piece of paper it is written on, and without DNA paternity testing there is no guar-antee that the sire is as stated on it. A great deal of trust is required, and the best way to ensure that the above problems are overcome is to buy a puppy from a reputable breeder/competitor. By attending sheepdog trials as a spectator you will get to know competitors and their dogs. Don't be afraid to ask questions, and talking to different handlers will enable you to make an informed choice about the right puppy for your needs. Also read lots of books, not just on training, but on health and breeding practice,

too. You might also want to find out whether you will be able to choose a particular pup from the litter. Many pups are sold or promised before they are born or grown up, especially from top competitors, and choice is not always possible. Remember it is your money, so spend it wisely.

Breeders vary immensely in their breeding practice, with some moving with the times and others following traditional practice, so always find out in advance how the litter will be reared. It is the responsibility of the breeder to ensure that puppies are well socialized, and grow up confident and bold; however, it is your responsi-bility to ensure that the puppy you choose reflects this. If you have any doubts whatsoever, listen to the voice in your head. This is not necessarily intuition: rather it is the voice of reason built on experience. You do not have to commit yourself to buying a particular pup. If you like someone and the information they give you, then this is a good start. Alternatively if a breeder does not have time for you, or seems to mind answering questions, then trust your own judgement. The more inexperienced you are, the more litters you should go and see so that you can develop an idea of the type of pup you like. Many breeders are happy for you to visit them more than once to see the pups, and this is a 'must'. Pups can be very lethargic when fed and sleep a lot, so depending on when you visit, what you see during the first visit might be totally different to the next visit. Question the breeder about their temperament, as he is best placed to offer you detailed information.

Dog or Bitch?

Whether you choose a dog or a bitch again depends on personal preference and circum-stances, although as you will discover later, the facts do speak for themselves. I have run both dogs and bitches over the years and have not been disappointed with either, where trials or

Portrait of a Successful Handler: John Ryan Griffiths

John Ryan Griffiths describes in his own words what it takes to become a successful handler and the types of dog which make successful sheepdogs.

I was born on a smallholding in Snowdonia, which is a hilly region of North Wales.

As soon as I could walk I would help my father with the sheep and cattle, so you could say that I have had experience of many different breeds of sheep all of my life.

I have, therefore, had years of experience with sheep, which gives you a greater understanding of the different breeds, and it helps when you need to 'read' sheep at trials.

My father had very little time for dogs, so the types he had were rough and ready and not up to the international standards needed for trials today. I remember going to local trials when I was a lad, when local farmers and the labourers would compete – looking back, the amount of money they won was very good – so the competition was very keen and intense.

When I was about twenty years of age I started buying dogs, which I would train and then sell on, but never went to sheepdog trials. When I was about twenty-four I became friends with Alan Jones, Pontllyfni, who was a very successful sheepdog handler in Wales. As Alan lived only a couple of miles from me I would often visit his farm and run dogs with him. He was a very good handler and I learnt a lot from watching him. I also went with Alan to many trials all over Wales and sometimes into England. I used to watch other top handlers, and studied carefully the way they handled their dogs on the course. I soon started to run dogs myself, and became addicted to trialling and training.

I don't think that luck has any part in being successful in sheepdog handling, just hard work and perseverance. But the most important thing that a trainer and handler needs is the right temperament. When you have so many different types of dog you have to be cool, and not become frustrated, training quietly at all times, and then when you do raise your voice the dogs know that you mean business.

What makes a successful dog? – that's the sixty-four thousand dollar question! A lot of the success depends on the handler – I have seen a lot of great dogs that I would love to have in the hands of

John Ryan Griffiths with the Nantlle Valley in the background.

other handlers who have not had any success with that particular dog. Also it depends a lot on the type of handler – a beginner might like a soft and easy dog, whilst a more experienced handler would not care if he had a stronger dog that takes much more handling.

In all my years as a dog breeder I think that the majority of pups that I have kept have been chosen by my wife. She is the one that looks after the pups from the day they are born, so she has first-hand knowledge of them. I do not have the temperament to wean the pups and to get them eating and keeping them clean. She will always choose a pup that is bold and not shy – one that will run up to you and not cower in the corner. It doesn't matter to me whether they are male or female.

Another important part of raising pups is the socializing – my wife is the one that gets them to go on a lead and also teaches them their names. I like them when they are older and ready for their first sight of the sheep – I love the excitement of seeing a pup showing interest in the sheep and seeing their potential as future international winners. Of course pups change so much – you may think that you have an international winner and then things change and you might be left with a good farm dog but not a trials dog.

I like a dog that is flexible, and a dog that is a good 'listener'. If you get a dog that 'listens' to you, you are halfway there before you start training. You may win more trials with a good 'listener' than with a better dog that wants to work his own way. My ideal dog would be the Wiston Cap type – a smart dog, rough-coated with prick ears. I dislike dogs with floppy spaniel ears and light eyes. I have yet to see a good ugly dog that was also a great dog.

(Courtesy John Ryan Griffiths, copyright holder)

Pups should be keen, alert and outgoing.

farm work are concerned. Many people, however, avoid bitches primarily because the trials calendar is often disrupted by them coming into season or nursing litters. Some bitches also change character when they are in pre-oestrus, as discussed before, and can run inconsistently, besides which at some trials they are not allowed to run until later in the day.

Depending on the lines you choose, some dogs can take longer to train than bitches; however, once trained they can sometimes offer greater consistency than bitches. What is an interesting fact, however, is that in the past fifty years only six bitches have won the International title, which is quite staggering. As a stark contrast, in the past fifty years forty-eight bitches have won the national from the home nations, as opposed to 152 dogs. Many handlers feel that in the long run dogs offer greater longevity and consistency, as well as a stronger presence and command over sheep, than bitches, although there are always exceptions to the rule.

Buying an Untrained Puppy or a Part-Trained Dog

There are many top handlers who neither like

training young dogs nor breeding their own. The late Alan Jones (Pontllyfni), for one, preferred to buy in part-trained dogs, or sent dogs for training and then had them back to fine tune them for trials. Alan was probably one of the most respected and successful triallists of all time. (Reference and information courtesy of Medwen Lloyd Jones.)

The major risk with buying a puppy is that there is no guarantee that it will work, and there is then the long wait for it to grow up before it is quick enough to keep up with the sheep. The advantage, however, of starting with a young pup is that you can shape and mould it exactly how you want. You can socialize it, and build up a bond with it, as well as undertake the early obedience training and generally build up a trusting relationship, which is crucial to sheep work. The biggest advantage of training your own puppy is that you will develop the skills to train your own dogs – and once you have trained one dog, training others will become that much easier. Of course you will make mistakes, but learning from them will make you a better trainer and handler.

Buying a ready-trained dog can bring benefits as well as problems. Having always been suspicious in nature I always question why anyone would want to sell a good dog. Of course not all dogs suit every handler, and some dogs may not have the right temperament to perform equally well on the farm as well as trials. Many handlers prefer strong dogs and will train and sell on softer, weekend-type dogs, namely those more suited to trialling. These days the price of quite mediocre dogs can reach £2,000, and it has been known for quite a bit more to be paid for dogs that really were not that special.

If you have spent a hefty sum purchasing a dog it is easy to assume and expect value for money. But remember, your dog does not know or care how much money has been spent acquiring it. It will work to its own agenda, and the more pressure you put on it to achieve

success quickly and bend it to your will, the more it will resist. Taking your time is the key to solving most problems. Buying dogs at dog sales can be risky; although I would always be happier buying a dog from someone that is a reputable trainer. A good trainer can often make a better job of a mediocre dog than a poor trainer can with a gifted dog. A dog that has varied experience of different sheep and terrain will also be an asset. Seeing a dog on home soil is always preferable as you can have longer to view the dog, and ask questions at your leisure.

Another good way of purchasing a trained dog is to follow the winter nursery trials over the course of a few months. This is the perfect opportunity to watch young dogs develop. It is always worth alerting a handler if you might be interested in purchasing their dog, if you especially like it – though you might also risk bidding the price up if you appear too keen or desperate. Buying a trained dog will also require time and patience while it becomes accustomed to your way of training. You will also need to learn the whistles it has been trained to or spend time retraining it.

You should also consider the age of the dog you are buying, taking into account the time it will take for you to get acquainted and address retraining issues or mistakes made by the previous owners. Most dogs are on borrowed time by the time they reach nine years of age, and keeping them fit and free of injury is crucial in prolonging their working life.

Whichever path you choose to take, whether it is with an older, trained dog or a young puppy, managing carefully their early experience and also their basic training will ensure success later on.

The next chapter looks at the importance of early training and socializing. This provides the building blocks for later, more advanced training on sheep and attending sheepdog trials. To be successful, handlers must have the willpower not only to win, but also to prepare and practise.

CHAPTER 2

EARLY TRAINING

WHAT AGE TO START?

There is no definitive answer to the question at what age you should start early training, as this depends on the tasks you are teaching, and the methods you intend to use to achieve them. Whatever the task, what is important is your puppy's ability to understand what you are trying to achieve, and to avoid any confusion. Puppies and older dogs will be far more willing to work for you if firstly, they have respect for you, and secondly they like you and have a bond with you. You must be seen to be fair and consistent in how you train, and above all I recommend a 'hands off' approach to all training. By this I mean that your hands must only be associated with positive actions such as stroking; if they are associated with force, pressure, grabbing or even smacking, dogs can become 'hand shy' and will avoid coming to you, or will be distracted by the consequences of your actions, rather than focusing on the task at hand.

As is the case with all aspects of training, there are always exceptions to the rule; however, the methods I am advocating are designed to minimize or avoid problems occurring in the future. I have always avoided the need to sell dogs that are not shaping up, or which have particular problems. Instead I try to understand why they are not performing to potential, preferring to put in place a plan to eradicate the particular problem, or sometimes more than one plan. Some plans work within days, while others can take longer. It is better not to set time frames and targets: leave that to the politicians. And if your dog makes a mistake, blame yourself for causing that mistake rather than labelling the dog as useless or stupid. The pleasure that is gained when a problem is solved is far greater than the pleasure of having money in your wallet for passing on the problem for someone else to resolve, especially if they succeed.

Before you ever take your dog to sheep there are a number of tasks that you have to achieve: lead training, the recall, the stand, the down and so on. By the time a puppy reaches the age of seven weeks they are already having adult brainwaves (Volhard 2009, *see* References) and are therefore ready to learn new concepts. This is a good time to introduce informal training, which can also serve to enforce dominance, a concept your puppy will already be familiar with from their mother.

LEAD AND COLLAR TRAINING

The period when lead training normally occurs – at eight to twelve weeks old – is generally the most stressful for puppies, particularly when you have bought the puppy from a breeder and they are not familiar with you or your home. They will have left their littermates and familiar surroundings; they may also have had a long car journey, which they may not be used to; a trip to the vet for vaccinations and eye tests; a change of diet, and so on. Most puppies will object to a lead and collar being placed on them, so it is better to introduce a collar at meal times when the puppy is distracted. Once they become used to wearing the collar, introduce a lead and generally allow the puppy to go wherever it wants to, within reason. (Note that it is only during this early stage that you would allow the puppy to go where it wants, or even to trail a lead for a short while.)

Once the puppy starts to accept the lead you can introduce a little food and encourage it to follow this. On rare occasions a puppy will resist quite violently, swinging erratically, but avoid using your hands to restrain it because it may use its teeth. Stay calm and focused, and the puppy will become more receptive to a food reward. It is also far better to remain silent and to 'ride the storm'. Any training done in anger will undoubtedly be flawed, and neither you nor your dog will enjoy the experience.

If your puppy comes to a halt and refuses to move, how you handle it is one of the most crucial aspects of early training that you will ever be responsible for. There are many reasons why a puppy refuses to move: however, if he is afraid of something, or is anxious, then the chances are that he has passive resistant tendencies (*see* Chapter 4) and this must be

---

Guiding Principle

Remember, whenever you speak to your dog it is worthwhile asking yourself 'Did he understand what I said?' If the answer is 'No', then it is far better to achieve the behaviour first and then put a command or name to the action.

---

stage managed to perfection otherwise he will come to realize your failings as a handler.

At the point where your puppy comes to a halt, pull him gently, avoiding any jerking, and keeping the pressure constant until he gets up and starts to move. At the exact moment he begins to walk, ease the pressure on the collar and use a treat to bait the puppy forwards and encourage him. Where possible avoid eye contact and turn your back on the pup, still maintaining a loose lead. Gradually through repetition your puppy will become more fluent and confident on the lead.

The collars I use when lead training are known as half-check collars. These collars are preferable to the ordinary webbed one-piece collar as they can be placed higher on to the dog's neck thereby avoiding any choking effect. They can also be loosened when the puppy is walking properly to heel. They are safer to use as they will almost certainly never come off your puppy's neck should it pull on the lead excessively. The other advantage of this type of collar is that because it slips over the puppy's head, all you have to do is hold it in front of a puppy with a treat in front of it: as the puppy reaches forwards to take the treat the collar will automatically slip over its head, thereby avoiding any negative conditioned response to the collar (*see* Chapter 8). When you are finished, remember to remove the collar to avoid accidents.

The sort of lead I like to use is about 1m long and ½in wide, with a light clip. Before clipping the lead to the collar I would give the puppy a treat and give the command 'Lead on'. Eventually the 'Lead on' command will also act as a recall command should you need it.

It is far better that puppies grow to like their lead and collar and associate them with something positive. Thereafter I recommend that all early training is carried out on the lead so the puppy can make fewer mistakes, cannot run off, and corrections can be made swiftly and at the appropriate time.

SOCIALIZATION

Socialization for working dogs, not just the ones that are to be trialled, is of the utmost importance. When handlers let out sheep they might wave their arms around, or their crooks, but what good is a dog if it is afraid of this? Some trials are held in conjunction with agricultural shows and often there is gunfire from clay pigeon shoots, or large crowds, or even marquees blowing in the wind. A dog that disregards all of these and shows strength of character in such circumstances will pay you back countless times. Even if the dog is not suited to trialling there might come a time when you decide to take it to a sheepdog sale. A dog's strength of character is something that everyone looks for, even before it is seen working. How many people select a pup that appears the boldest?

If you have chosen to buy in a puppy, you can save yourself many problems by ensuring that the breeder has carefully controlled its upbringing. Most breeders will be willing to sell puppies at around six or seven weeks old, by which time they will have been weaned to solid foods and also away from their mother. Before this period the time that the puppies spend with their mother is probably the most crucial in determining their personalities. Once the puppy's eyes and ear canals are opened they will start to play with one another and their mother. It is also the mother's duty to ensure that she stimulates the puppies to defecate and keep them clean. She is neither gentle nor careful in performing these grooming tasks, nor is she careful when she leaves their bed or returns to it and will often tread on a puppy, which will let out a loud scream. But mothers are matter-of-fact, and confident: she will do exactly what she wants with the puppies, and they learn to accept all types of handling from her without too much objection.

Experts have reported that bitches nursing a litter of puppies frequently release a pheromone into the air, which ensures that puppies feel safe, secure and protected at times of stress. It is generally believed that pheromones are used to communicate between the same species. I would hypothesize that familiarity between humans and dog, or indeed sheep and dogs, or even sheep and humans can lead to a common ground, the end result being trust in one another. These days, artificially manufactured pheromones are readily available in pet shops and veterinary surgeries; they are commonly know as DAP ('Dog Appeasement Pheromone') diffusers (*see* Chapter 6).

Socialization is not about introducing your dog to as many situations as possible: it is what you do during a social encounter that matters, and the best way to socialize your dog is to maintain informality yet control, be this with other dogs or people, or in any situation.

Socialization Exercise

Apply the 'no pull rule' as follows: whenever your puppy pulls towards anything – be it a dog, sheep, child, adult, farm gate – it is your duty to ensure that he does not succeed. Just hold him back – no command is needed – and he will do one of the following: stop pulling, sit, lie down, or relax the lead and remain standing.

As soon as he does one of the above, keeping the lead loose or looped, and using the command 'Off you go,' walk towards the person or dog you wish your puppy to meet.

Allow them to meet for about five seconds, and then call your puppy back using his name and the command 'Come here', or 'That'll do', or 'That's enough'. If he ignores your instruction then use the lead and make him come back to you, giving him a titbit on his return. Repeat this as often as you like.

A dog that is allowed to learn any task without interference from his human counterpart will develop its own strength of character. In life, to develop strength of character you have to be allowed the opportunity to fight your own battles, and this is true of human and animal. If your young puppy comes across something that causes it anxiety or is frightening, he must be allowed to develop his own coping strategies, rather than his owners stepping in and taking over. Your role should be simply to be there with your puppy and do nothing. If you stay calm, your puppy will soon realize that there is nothing to worry about. If, however, you reassure your puppy that everything will be OK *whilst they are in a state of anxiety* – and if you even go as far as stroking him – then what you will achieve and reward *is a state of anxiety*. If your puppy comes to no harm, that is all the information he needs – namely not to be afraid, if and when the situation next arises.

Quite simply, by not articulating, when faced with something that invokes a fear response, you are negating its impact on you. For instance, before Jo and I had children she was absolutely petrified of spiders, to the point of screaming when she saw one and refusing to stay in the same room. Once Kieran and Laura were born, Jo realized that she had to set an example, and refrained from screaming. If the children saw a spider, in order to prevent them from becoming frightened of it she would give it a name, such as 'George' or 'Fred'. Once the spider had a name, it seemed to take on a less threatening and terrifying persona. A few months later, although Jo never got to the stage where she would pick up a spider, she did nevertheless manage to avoid the hysterics we had become accustomed to.

In many situations, whether it is with children or animals, it is because of our desperate need to provide a caring and loving role that we overstep the mark, when what is really called for is 'tough love'.

When puppies or even older dogs are on the lead and are faced with a situation that invokes fear, it is the handler's duty to ensure that once the dog is under control the lead is held loose and has a loop in it. Like this, any tension that the handler is feeling remains firmly with them. If a handler identifies that someone or something might pose a threat and instinctively tightens the lead and keeps it tight, then the puppy or adult dog will come to associate a tight lead with problems, and will react accordingly in an undesirable manner. This may take the form of barking, pulling or snarling. It is your duty to disassociate yourself from any behaviour that is irrational, otherwise your dog may develop a phobia.

For this reason it is essential that your dog is exercised off the lead so that it learns to trust in you as the pack leader. By allowing your dog to walk off the lead it will learn about dominance and submission, two skills that will keep it safe from more dominant and unfriendly dogs. In most situations that invoke fear either in the dog or the handler, our response is a totally irrational one. We cannot let one negative experience pave the way for the future. As the old adage goes: 'If you fall off your bike, you must get right back on again.' However, care should be taken as to the safety of your dog as well as other animals.

These days it is quite common for triallists to bring their young pups to sheepdog trials; I have even seen whole litters of pups running around at trials, and although sometimes I have cringed when a pup has run up to a chained, unfriendly dog, I have yet to see one come to any harm. On the whole pups are very astute as to which dogs are friendly and which are not.

Socializing Car Chasers

Although socializing dogs with traffic is a good idea in theory, and getting them used to busy roads, the only exception to this rule is when you have a puppy that is a serious car chaser. Unfortunately, the only way to determine whether a dog is a car chaser is to first expose them to traffic, just as farmers or triallists try their young dogs on sheep for the first time to gauge their reaction. Once you know your dog will work it is simply a matter of giving them time to mature before starting any formal work with them. The same is true for dealing with car chasers. It is always worth asking breeders if their particular breeding lines have thrown car chasers in the past.

Almost every dog I have bred has chased cars, and I have been in a position to forewarn new owners of this. I have known young dogs, whilst off the lead, to suddenly take off after a car and to nearly get themselves run over. Great care needs to be taken when letting this type of dog off the lead near traffic. The solution with all of them is to walk them either well away from traffic, or where there is limited traffic or none at all. As with sheep work, when the pups are later introduced to traffic their reaction will be less intense and not such a problem, because they will have developed better coping strategies from other, similar situations, as well as having grown up. This is consistent with the 'Concept of Opposites' mentioned later in the book (*see* p. 128).

Early training, as discussed earlier, is very important; however, trying to effect a gradual

Tip
■ If you are not confident enough to let your dog off the lead, then it will consequently ignore you or disobey you in all difficult situations.
■ If your dog is visibly frightened in any situation, do not reassure it or give it any reinforcement for that particular behaviour as this reaction will become habitual.
■ Trust your dog and it will repay you many times over. Mistrust your dog and it will simply ignore you, run away, have poor recalls, and in general will acquire a very aloof disposition.

change from a dog's perspective requires understanding and patience. Training and communicating with your dog in a manner that is consistent with its upbringing will ensure that you have a willing student who embraces your teaching with enthusiasm.

Before you can move on to more advanced training with your dog it is essential that you have a good understanding of each other. The age-old concept of dominance is discussed in the next chapter. The issues surrounding dominance have caused a great deal of confusion as well as debate, but are clarified to reveal a most simplistic process of communicating with your Border Collie.

CHAPTER 3

THE DOMINANCE DEBATE

INTRODUCTION TO DOMINANCE

Dominance is not about who is bigger or stronger, although this is sometimes the case. You are merely setting up an environment that enables you to control access to something your dog desires, and they have to look to you to get what they want.

Dominance conveys a set of rules and a structure by which dogs live within a social context, and how these rules are expressed or communicated by higher ranking pack members through both sound and non-verbal communication. As a natural pack leader it is your role to set the rules and have expectations about how your dog must behave. Consistency is the key to this.

Rules and limits have to be the focal point of any relationship with dogs, as they inform them that there is a system in place, the manner in which it operates, and what is expected. Only once rules have been established is it then rational to apply consequences.

Rules and boundaries are the linchpin for a stable relationship: lacking any rules there would be an assumption that all species are equal. As was the case in George Orwell's novel *Animal Farm*, first, all animals are equal; however, class and status disparities soon emerge between the different animal species (the pigs being the 'greater species'). To quote George

Orwell: 'All animals are equal, some animals are more equal than others' (Orwell 1996).

MISCONCEPTIONS ABOUT DOMINANCE

There is a great deal written on the subject of dominance or pack leadership, and in some respects the 'politically correct brigade' has turned something that is very natural among many species into something which they see as negative and undesirable. Even within the context of my dog club I tread carefully so as not to upset people who associate dominance with being cruel or harsh, as something that is unnecessary and has no place in the dog world. Many authors have offered simplistic views about 'old generation dog trainers' upholding the dominance theory through physical means only through an actual struggle. Yet this is furthest from the truth as I see it. For any species to gain control through force and aggression solely would be folly, and would not ensure survival or peace of mind. The most violent of all species is man. We smack our children, we fight in wars and we kill our own. It is our nature to fight and kill, and we have been doing so since time began. The concept of dominance is no more outdated than is Charles Darwin's theory of evolution!

Misconceptions about dominance probably occurred because the word 'dominance' does not convey a positive meaning, as would the term 'dog psychology' or similar. Some people have also misconstrued the meaning of dominance and taken the meaning more literally, using more forceful or sometimes aggressive methods of training. Even on the trials field I have heard people pass on advice such as 'You've got to show the dog who is boss'; or – joke, I hope – 'He stopped gripping once he felt the lead pipe.' Fortunately this type of handler is very much an exception. Some dogs might well cope with heavy handedness better than others, but this does not make it right. Training a sheepdog is no different to raising a child: it should be a labour of love, and not a stretch at Guantanamo Bay!

'TREAT THEM WITH A LITTLE BIT OF KINDNESS'

Having been brought up both laughing and crying at the genius of Laurel and Hardy, I have always remembered a line from the film *Brats*

when Oliver Hardy advises Stan Laurel how to parent: 'Treat them with a little bit of kindness and you'll get more out of them.' The same applies to dogs. This does not mean that you cannot be firm, however. Working dogs, like athletes, need pushing to achieve peak performance, and many runners or sportsmen, for example, will tell you that whilst training they sometimes 'reach the wall', a psychological state where the mind and body feel they cannot go any further. Once they are pushed beyond this, however, they find a new level of consciousness that provides greater energy and a more positive mindset.

There are many schools of thought that devalue the importance of dominance, dismissing the similarities of dog behaviour to wolf behaviour as myths. They suggest that dog trainers who concur with the theory of dominance believe 'that animals that misbehave do so in order to strive for a higher rank'.

I have also heard theories that wolves were hunters and dogs evolved into scavengers.

A close relative of the wolf?

Hunting as a pack.

However, if it were as clear cut as this, breeds such as Border Collies would not be so adept at herding sheep, and there would be no cases of dogs attacking, worrying and killing sheep on farms. One also needs to consider carefully the fact that many of the attacks by dogs on humans involve children.

If bad or unacceptable behaviour remains unchallenged, then this will result in the owner losing not only respect, but also their higher rank; the dog will then move up the pecking order, as a consequence of their success. In short, behaviours occur because they are reinforced either by the owner or by the dog achieving success in any given task. Initially the gaining of a higher rank is coincidental. However, once a dog is successful in a given task, this will then spur it on further to achieve yet greater success. For example, if a dog learns to run off to the sheep at the end of a training session, due to the owner's failure to place it on a lead, it will repeatedly run off back to the sheep. It may also run to the sheep prematurely, at the start of an outrun before the handler has got into the correct position. Dogs will also be more likely to resist any subsequent challenges to relinquish their new-found status.

Once behaviour becomes established, it is nevertheless possible to retrain a dog through positive reinforcement. Where humans are concerned, in many cases dogs don't need to behave badly to achieve a higher rank as some people are quite happy to step aside, through ignorance or by humanizing the situation, and offer a higher ranking position to their dogs. The same is sadly true for some people who, rather than being parents to their children, would prefer to be their friends. Some people are good at giving instruction, whereas others are better at receiving it. Also some people do not like to take on a leadership role as it makes them feel uncomfortable. However, when you obtain a puppy or adult dog you lose the rights to choose whether to be leader or not.

Gregory (1988) offered the following four 'I's, where humans are directly responsible for the suffering of animals:

Ignorance – Either not knowing or claiming not to know what to do.
Inexperience – Not knowing how to do something despite knowing what needs doing.
Incompetence – Lacking the ability to perform a task.
Inconsideration – Lacking in compassion and sensitivity.

WHO IS THE REAL OFFENDER?

The majority of problems that I deal with are caused by people who, as human beings and out of ignorance, think that it is appropriate and acceptable to apply human psychology to dogs. This is similar to those of us who go abroad on holiday and assume that the locals will speak English, rather than making the effort to speak their language. When we interact with one another, it is based on factors such as the emotions – love, politeness and rudeness, to mention a few. Interaction between dogs is based on less complicated concepts such as ownership and strength, and of course access, all conveyed through smell or energy, and posture.

Whenever we are faced with problems with dogs we often fail to recognize that we may have caused them. Sometimes, rather than trying to alter your dog's behaviour, it may actu-

ally be far simpler to try to alter your own and try to understand the reasons that caused your dog to misbehave or ignore you. It is a distinctly human trait to expect others, whether they are people from a different background or culture, race or another species, to fit in with our way of life. We try and mould people and animals to extensions of ourselves rather than accept them for what they are. Of course there will always be some common ground, but on the whole the differences far outweigh the similarities.

The reason we instinctively look at things from a human perspective is quite simply because that is what we are. However, if man is supposed to be more intelligent than his animal counterpart then it also makes sense to alter one's way of thinking, and to try and at least attempt to imagine what life is like from a dog's perspective.

THE NEED FOR CONSISTENCY

There are two ways in which you can change your dog's behaviour: through obedience and dominance. Whenever people bring their dogs to me for training, their aim is for their dog to become more obedient. For me, dominance has always been the first option I explore in trying to alter behaviour. I view obedience as teaching your puppy the English language, which is a longer term option. What most people desire is to be able to use a number of words or short phrases and for the dog to carry out the instruction quickly and efficiently. Dominance, on the other hand, is about understanding why dogs behave the way they do, what motivates them, and why and how they function as a pack animal. Dominance is a set of rules by which dogs live, and overall the rules are far less flexible than the ones people live by. We change with the wind depending on mood, health, convenience and sometimes inclination.

Any process that involves change has the potential for causing stress to a puppy or dog, so

CONTROLLING ACCESS

Below is a list of privileges as seen through your dog's eyes. Depending on whether your dog is kennelled or lives in the house as a member of your family, some of them will either not apply or will hold less significance for you. The first category consists of general privileges, when you allow your dog:

- To jump up to greet you.
- To bark excessively.
- To pull on the lead unchallenged.
- To jump on the furniture.
- To go upstairs, especially in the bedroom and on the bed.
- To follow you around the house or pester you for attention.
- To stop during lead walks to sniff or to cock its leg to mark territory.
- To barge past you in narrow spaces, through doors, or farm gateways.
- To misbehave, and fail to respond in any way.
- To mouth, bite or nip.

The second category consists of privileges for the working dog, when you allow him:

- To be around or with stock without supervision.
- To walk first into a training pen or field with sheep.
- To walk in front of you whilst approaching sheep or cattle.
- To barge his way out of the car prior to working sheep or cattle.
- To eye sheep excessively without breaking contact.
- To use predatory or aggressive eye contact or behaviour, while failing to respond or object.
- To bark excessively, whilst kennelled or otherwise, without challenging him.

I have heard many experts suggest that some of the points mentioned above are 'way off the mark' in terms of pack rules; however, what they fail to point out is that they can only be deemed to be irrelevant if there are no consequences of allowing those behaviours to take place. Neither dogs nor humans are dominant all the time: they are dominant only when it matters and when something is at stake. Allowing a dog to go first through a door into the garden may not have any consequences, but allowing him to go through the front door unsupervised may lead to a hefty veterinary bill. Many farm dogs are chained up because of their own safety and the safety of farm animals. Dogs running around busy farm machinery are a liability, and dogs that chase and kill ducks and hens need to have restricted or controlled access. Allowing a young dog unrestricted access into a field full of sheep would certainly be irresponsible.

WHAT MY DOG THINKS ABOUT ME

It is important to realize that dogs do not exhibit the above behaviours in order to obtain a higher rank, and individually these scenarios may not promote your dog towards a higher rank. Dogs also don't consciously try to wind you up. However, the particular behaviours may provide the starting block for a stronger and more intense response the next time you and the dog reach a state of conflict. There may also be a cumulative effect of your dog achieving success, which may lead to greater resistance to any change that is demanded by you.

I recall a farmer allowing his young dog to work his sheep without supervision, whilst he worked on repairing some fencing nearby. As the dog was seemingly doing no harm and showed great restraint in moving the sheep around the two-acre field, he saw no reason to prevent this. The dog took it on itself to ensure that the sheep were held to the farmer, and prevented them from leaving the field into a nearby paddock. However, having allowed this young dog to work unsupervised, when it came to fine tuning the dog for trials in the very same field, it had become so accustomed to working in its own way – its instinct to predict the sheep's movement and hold them to the handler had intensified – that it strongly resisted any directions from the farmer to do anything to the contrary, seeing them as a challenge. The dog would take up a position that always brought the sheep to the farmer, and would only flank in the direction that prevented the sheep from escaping into the next field. This problem took several weeks to eradicate, and had the dog been prevented from having free and unre-

stricted access to the sheep this would not have become such an arduous task. The only good thing to come out of this was the lesson that was learnt, as the farmer made quite sure that his dogs were never left unattended with sheep again.

In the canine world leadership is never shared, therefore the more a dog is allowed to get away with bad behaviour, the more likely it is to disregard you as a leader. This might occur over a period of time, during which your dog will gradually become less obedient and more challenging of anything you say. This defiance may provoke you into becoming angry or even aggressive – but this behaviour will merely serve to inform the dog that his actions are working. In many cases where people become angry or

---

Case Study – Mike and Filbert

In 2008 a Border Collie by the name of Filbert and his owner Mike came to me for training. During one of the early sessions Filbert refused to stay in the down position so Mike walked up to him and held his collar. As Filbert was generally a trustworthy dog, he was not used to being controlled by a lead and collar, even though on this occasion his collar was attached to a long line. When Mike held the collar, Filbert objected by mouthing his hand; Mike held on, and this caused Filbert to resist quite violently, trying to wriggle free, and again he tried to bite Mike in an attempt to avoid the close control. Mike informed me that this had happened previously on his farm when he had tried to take Filbert away from some hens.

This behaviour is quite typical of a dog that is 'passive resistant' (*see* Chapter 4). It will refuse to do something, whether jump into the car or go into a kennel, and if force is used then its response can become aggressive. Greater tact is called for, but the difficulty arises in knowing

what to do when the dog becomes aggressive. In Filbert's case Mike continued to restrict Filbert's movement towards the sheep, and for about a minute Filbert resisted by trying to escape from the lead quite violently.

I advised Mike to stand perfectly still in an upright stance, and continue to hold firm, not pulling or jerking the lead in any way, and to remain calm and avoid saying anything. Within a minute of doing this Filbert snapped out of his rage and totally forgot anything that had gone on before, and was now happy to oblige by lying down until Mike was ready to send him on his outrun. Had Mike become embroiled in Filbert's outburst it would merely have served to fuel his resistance; by staying calm he signalled to Filbert that he was in control. Also by virtue of his calmness, Mike would have secreted calm pheromones into the air, which Filbert would have smelled and responded to.

(Information courtesy of Mike Birch.)

aggressive with their dogs in response to their bad behaviour, it is the dogs that have caused you to press a metaphorical 'self-destruct' button – and once this button is pressed, the dog's behaviour will not get better, but worse. If you force the issue by grabbing at them or their collar, it is at this point that they will choose to use their teeth, in a very instinctive way, to persuade you to back down. This is a quite common phenomenon, and something that I come across with great regularity.

Many of the privileges stated earlier involve physical height – for example, a dog that is allowed to climb the stairs, jump on the bed or settee, or cock its leg to ensure a scent is marked off ground level to ensure longevity. Height is an important factor in determining dominance, which is why dogs, when in the presence of other dogs, will make themselves look more upright, with head up, ears erect, chest out and so on.

In the photographs you can see my dog Mac with a mule ewe. Following a run at a trial when Mac's lift was extremely aggressive, I decided to put him in a situation that would invoke predatory behaviour, but where he was also under strong pressure to resist any aggression, because I was there to intervene. The photos were taken a few minutes apart, and you can see that there is concern on his face in the picture on the left, whereas the picture on the right shows him to be more relaxed. I do believe that whether the issue involves people from different races or animals of differing species, it is possible for all concerned to live in peace and harmony and without conflict. The only prerequisites to achieving success are willingness from both parties, determination, and plenty of time.

SIMILARITY IN THOUGHT PROCESS BETWEEN CHILDREN AND DOGS

In some respects many analogies can be drawn between raising puppies and raising children. Children need rules and boundaries, and they need both parents to sing from the same 'hymn sheet' or they will play one off against the other. They require a parent who instils confidence in them when they become frightened so they believe that all will end well, and they need love and guidance. Both children and puppies can also, of course, be spoilt. However, on the whole I find that people have a greater intolerance to bad behaviour from children than from dogs. It is also my experience that people who have strong leadership roles as part of their profession, such as doctors or social workers often make the worst dog trainers or disciplinarians as they do not wish to practise their work role or leadership role in their spare time. There are always, however, exceptions to the rule.

There is also some common ground in terms of how children and dogs think. Consider the following scenario: a child is left in a room with some cakes and sweets, left on a coffee table. Prior to leaving the room the child is told by a parent 'Whatever you do, don't touch the cakes!' On their return, there is a good chance the sweets will have gone but the cakes will remain untouched. When the child is asked what happened to the sweets, the following responses might be given:

- I don't know what happened to the sweets!
- You said don't eat the cakes!
- You didn't say don't touch the sweets!

The message here is quite clear: if you don't want something to occur you have to be prepared to spell it out. Therefore the instructions that should have been given were 'Don't touch the sweets or the cakes!' Similarly, if you don't want your dog to behave in a particular way, then it is your duty to make it clear each time that there is a threat of that behaviour occurring. This does not mean, however, that you will succeed each time.

ABOVE: *Predatory look turns to curiosity.*   BELOW: *You're not so frightening after all!*

ABOVE: We really ought to make the first move.   *BELOW:* And they all lived happily ever after.

DEALING WITH THOUGHTS RATHER THAN BEHAVIOUR

There are many instances when a dog will do something wrong and you will say to yourself 'I knew that was going to happen!' If you know something undesirable might occur, then you need to state your objection to the dog at the very point at which you reach that decision. People often refer to intuition when it comes to predicting the future; however, intuition is simply based on experience of past events, or events that are easy to predict. So for example, when a dog sees sheep in a field, it is not surprising when he pulls you through a gateway to get to them; even when your dog cannot see the sheep, he can smell them. If you can predict that your dog will pull on the lead, then you should command him not to do so before he does.

When it comes to training there are many situations that are predictable, and when faced with these situations you are more likely to succeed in stopping or eradicating poor behaviour if you command your dog – for example with a stop command – when you first suspect that it might be about to misbehave. If you are too late and the poor behaviour manifests itself, then all is not lost, because if you give a stop command within the first two seconds of the behaviour being observed you will stand a good chance of succeeding in stopping your dog's behaviour altogether. As in all cases, however, there is no room for inconsistency, and you should learn to watch your dog, because there is always a clue as to how they intend to behave in how or where they look, or whether their ears become erect, or the change in intensity in their eyes.

Any given behaviour can be viewed in terms of a scale of zero to ten, where zero represents your dog thinking about misbehaving, one represents low intensity, and ten represents high intensity. It is far better to deal with a dog at level zero or one, before it becomes highly motivated or aroused by a given situation or stimuli. Should you find that you are slow to react, or fail to react quickly enough, the only thing left to do is to physically stop the dog pulling or chasing by restricting its lead first and then giving a 'stand' or 'get back' command. In a working situation where the dog may not be on a lead, then physical pressure needs to be applied (*see* Chapter 9). Once the dog stops, then the lead or pressure can be loosened or withdrawn and the responsibility placed on the dog to behave appropriately. But remember: if you continue to hold the lead tight or fail to withdraw pressure, your dog will not be a willing participant and will not learn anything.

ACHIEVING DOMINANCE IN A PRACTICAL SETTING

The Lead and Collar

The majority of dog handlers make use of some form of dog lead or leash, and in some cases a long line. How the lead is used determines whether a dog feels empowered, or whether the handler is empowered. A lead should only be used briefly, for correction purposes. It matters very little whether it is you who tightens the lead or your dog: a tight lead is a tight lead. Once a young pup has been taught the 'no pull rule' (*see* Chapter 8), the only time you should make a correction is when it attempts to pull, or when you think it is about to pull. Whilst the pup is not pulling you should offer a totally loose lead and put the responsibility on to the pup to behave, rather than take on the responsibility yourself.

In the same way as dogs are not dominant for every second of the day, you should only take on a dominant role when it is called for. Therefore, a loose lead implies you are in charge because the dog is doing all the work, and a tight lead implies that the dog is in charge.

There is nothing wrong with using the lead to make a correction, however as soon as the desired behaviour is achieved then it should be loosened once more. The same is true when using a long line.

Going Through a Farm Gate

When going through a farm gate, doorway or any narrow space, it is not enough that you tighten the dog's lead and stop him from going ahead of you. Bearing in mind the advice given above, it is far better that you place your dog on a loose lead and use your body to block him, applying pressure on the dog by walking towards him and releasing it again. Even where no command is given, your dog will stay if the correct amount of pressure has been applied. Once your dog sits, stands perfectly still, or lies down, you can then invite or call him in, but if his approach is rushed, then you will need to apply pressure again. Once your dog gets the idea it will walk at a slower pace, rather than barge past. Similarly, teaching your dog in this way to pace when working sheep will enable you to control his chase instinct and subsequently the instinct to kill sheep.

FACTORS THAT CAN AFFECT DOMINANCE

The following factors can all affect dominance and cause a change in the hierarchy:

- **Hormones:** Bitches that are undergoing hormonal changes due to being in the pre-oestrus cycle can find hidden strengths in their character. Dogs, too, can become more aggressive or challenging, or lack concentration in their work.
- **Seasons:** Bitches in season, as above, can not only move up in the hierarchy but also cause acts of sporadic aggression between males that are not castrated.
- **Litter:** Bitches nursing a litter as well as those expecting puppies can undergo hormonal changes resulting in hierarchical changes.
- **False pregnancy.**

PUPPIES AND DOMINANCE

Most of us find it very difficult, whether dealing with people or animals, to stay silent. We feel awkward when there is silence, and tend to fill the void with nonsense such as talking about the weather. Where your puppies are concerned, the less you say, the less chance there is that you will confuse them. It is better to put words to actions they are performing so they learn to associate their behaviour with particular sounds or commands. If they do something you don't like, you can ignore that and by using the lead and collar, prevent it from happening again.

The reason I favour dominance is because puppies normally receive their first education from their mother as soon as they are born. This education serves to protect them, ensures their survival, and enables them to lead a trouble-free life within a pack. If you continue in the same vein your puppy will settle in well and will be just as obedient, if not more so. There is absolutely no point in focusing on the English language to the exclusion of anything else if your puppy comes to you already equipped with a good understanding of dominance. In my experience, dominance works far more quickly than teaching a dog to understand the English language. Dominance involves elements of dog psychology, and there is no room for punishment or heavy-handedness, although your puppy will take full advantage of your physical inabilities or weak mental state.

You only have to observe a litter of puppies with their mother. Mum can achieve a far greater degree of obedience from six or seven puppies using simple body postures or movements, and eye contact or simple growls, than we can with one puppy. Imagine a scenario whereby a mother is eating her food. If one of the puppies from her litter decides that it is hungry it may decide to move towards the mother in the hope that she might share some food. As soon as the mother notices and becomes aware of the puppy's intentions, she will glare at the puppy with a fixed stare. If the puppy fails to recognize this signal she will then combine a fixed stare with a deep growl. If both audible and visual signals fail and the puppy still continues to move towards the mother, the next and final action will be of a swift touch or bite around the neck area. If the puppy survives, it most certainly will not repeat this behaviour, and will learn from it; if it does not survive it may well be that its failure to respond to the signals was because it was deaf and blind. The message that the mother conveys in this scenario is to do with ownership: everything belongs to her unless she indicates otherwise – she is controlling access.

As the pups are weaned on to solid food, they are often fed from a big dish together. This teaches them to be competitive, and if certain puppies do not eat the food quickly enough then they go hungry. However, over the last few years I have changed from this practice because I have noticed that pups of my breeding are highly motivated by food and it has caused them to develop guarding behaviour. Instead I feed them in pairs, so there is still an element of competition, but it is less intense. However, only in some situations has this policy been successful in eradicating the guarding behaviour.

The ideal structure for mealtimes should be for all dogs to eat together with you, as the pack leader, present to ensure there is no excitement or indeed resulting aggression or guarding behaviour. Many theorists of dominance used to postulate that the top dog should be given his food first, then the next dog in rank, and so on. However, I have found that it is far better to reward behaviour that is calm and free of excitement or aggression. Whether you are feeding pups or adults, each dog should be asked to 'lie down' or 'stand still' before being given its food, and then given permission to 'take it'. This has the advantage of teaching the more excitable dogs, and even the aggressive ones, that they do not merit getting their food until they have reduced their high level of energy and reached a state of calm. It also ensures that they are less predatory. Where younger dogs are concerned it gives you the opportunity to practise the stop commands for later work.

The same theory can be applied when you take your dogs out, either to train or to carry out your daily shepherding tasks. You will notice that some dogs are keener than others to get on with the job, whilst others are happy to wait their turn until they are asked. To reward this calm type of dog will very quickly signal to those that are excited that their heightened level of energy merely serves to delay their opportunity to work.

I recall many years ago visiting J. R. Griffiths (Talysarn) following the International at Chatsworth House in the Derbyshire Peak District in 1996. Having walked a few metres from his home down to a small field of about three or four acres, we stood on the bank of a small hill. He sent Moss and Sweep to the right through a gateway to gather a few Welsh Mountain ewes. The comparison between this field and running at Chatsworth a few weeks previously was immense. As John continued to bring the sheep nearer to him I asked him how he had managed to achieve such wonderful outruns at Chatsworth, yet his dogs were only used to running in small fields. His response quite took me by surprise: 'It's all about attitude. Before starting out on their outrun make sure that your dog has no attitude, and they will run out better. It doesn't matter how small the fields are that you work in.' What John meant is that before a dog runs, its mind should be blank, empty of any preconceived ideas. This will then enable it to run out wider and process any information it comes across in a calm and controlled manner in order to find and gather the sheep. (Information courtesy of John Ryan Griffiths.)

PASSIVE DOMINANCE

The dominance theory has been used extensively by many dog behaviour practitioners and trainers to explain and find solutions for many problems. However, it is also important to recognize the significance of passive dominance.

Passive dominance occurs where dogs behave in a sly or subtle manner that enables them to effect change in their owners. Often the owners are not aware that the dog is manipulating them because their intentions are not obvious or apparent. I believe that dogs cannot be categorized as dominant or passive dominant; however, all dogs have an element of both, and it is the degree to which each type predominates that is of significance.

There are many situations where dogs get their own way by inadvertently looking cutely into our eyes, by sheer persistence, or by only partially following instructions, to con us into thinking that they have been obedient. For example, a farmer might ask his dog to lie down whilst he lambs a ewe. The dog may creep forwards, and although when asked will temporarily move away, a few seconds later it continues to come closer and investigate what he is doing, as if it has no recollection of being asked to keep away. To avoid being told off the dog might even lie down and look inconspicuous or avert its eyes. In some cases the farmer will succumb and allow the dog to remain as long as no harm is caused.

I had first hand experience of passive dominance from my old dog Jade, who was quite the expert at the art of human manipulation. I was to discover that there were other elements to dog behaviour that could not be neatly categorized or explained by the dominance theory, either active or passive. In some cases these elements of behaviour defied the dominance theory. They followed consistent themes, and it became relatively easy to predict behaviour problems that would result by handling dogs in a particular way, given certain situations. Jo and I decided to categorize these under a new concept, which we called 'passive resistance'.

CHAPTER 4

THE PASSIVE RESISTANCE THEORY

MY INTRODUCTION TO PASSIVE RESISTANCE

In 1996 I purchased a Border Collie puppy, Fly, from North Wales following the death of my young dog Moss due to epilepsy. There were plenty of warnings as to why I should not buy Fly, none more so than that her litter brother was returned to the breeder because he was aggressive towards people, particularly children. However, Fly was similarly bred to my Moss, whose sire was J. R. Griffiths' Moss (188389) – and my judgement was clouded by emotion. John's Moss accompanied his litter brother Sweep to the Supreme Doubles title on two occasions. This was to become the start of a whole new chapter in my knowledge of dogs. Fly was to teach me more about dogs and their behaviour than any other dog I had owned, and in doing so, threw my understanding of dominance into total disarray. However, having her also introduced a new concept for me, that of 'passive resistance'.

When she was nine weeks old I took Fly to my dog club, and as she was unvaccinated, held her in my arms. We were approached by another owner and their dog, upon which Fly wriggled in my arms and bit me on the nose, quite instinctively and without provocation. Such an act of aggression didn't occur again for quite some time, and Fly behaved just as a plain Border Collie, easy going and friendly with everyone in the household. She was great with the children, who were both under ten years old; however, none of the dogs took to her for quite some time, despite her being a puppy.

It wasn't long before we observed that Fly was sensitive to church bells, and howled, quite sweetly, as though singing. She also howled when the telephone and doorbell rang.

Despite being at the bottom of the pack and the youngest, Fly demonstrated a strong food guarding instinct, and none of the higher ranking dogs in my household ever attempted to eat from her bowl whilst she was eating – they didn't dare go near her, such was her ferocity in defending her food. Moreover her reaction with strange dogs, where food was concerned, was a whole lot more aggressive, and sometimes she would go into attack mode without offering any warning whatsoever. Her reactions where food was concerned were very instinctive, and based, I felt, on strong survival instincts.

Otherwise she enjoyed chasing and fetching a ball, and proved easy to train for obedience and subsequently sheep work; indeed, once food was taken out of the equation, Fly became a normal, calm and friendly dog. She paid little or no attention to the ducks and rabbits that ran free in the garden. On the farm or on walks she was the greatest of scavengers, always on the lookout for food. If she found a dead ewe or lamb in the field she would never consider it as food unless another animal, probably badger or

Fly, aged twelve, showing her battle scar.

fox, had torn into it first: then it was fair game, and 'hers' at that. If the animal had not long died she would respect this and continue on her way; but if it were alive and in distress she was the first to sense this, and would offer comfort by lying by its side.

Fly's Training on Sheep

At seven months old I began training Fly on sheep. I had selected her lines carefully, having admired John Griffiths' two dogs for many years for their strong character and positive working style. But unfortunately with Fly I found I had got the opposite. She was easy to train and calm with sheep, but showed too much eye (*see* Chapter 12) for my liking. Although she never stopped short on her outrun, she nevertheless had far too much respect for sheep than I liked in my dogs. Her flanks, unlike her outrun, were painfully slow and wide. I could never get her to grip the sheep, although she would happily walk up to an old ewe and lick her on the nose. If, however, she felt threatened she would fully raise her top lip to reveal her pink jaw and full set of top teeth, though never resorted to a full blown attack. On the other hand, she chose to make a lot of noise, a sort of a growly, high-pitched bark. Where cattle were concerned, however, Fly was altogether different: strong, quick and powerful, happy to obey the 'take hold' command and nip at their feet, and if one faced up to her she was equally positive and would nip at its face.

Moving Up the Pecking Order

As my other dogs Jade and Lara grew old, Fly quite naturally moved up the pecking order and slept in the kitchen for a period of three years. It became noticeable that whenever we had visitors she would happily greet them, but would then go out of the lounge and always lie by the kitchen door. The kitchen is where she slept, and beyond the kitchen is the utility where she was, and still is fed, and where her food is kept. She began to view the kitchen as her territory, though was never territorial with either Jo, the children or me.

As regards the other dogs, however, she was a real 'madam'. She would slither, keeping her body low, almost crawling on her belly, to any canine pack member wishing to enter the kitchen, at the same time revealing her top teeth and gums and snarling, moving frenetically from side to side, blocking their entry into the kitchen. She would carry her head higher than her body and level with that of the other dog, giving it full, intense, wolf-like eye contact. She would only pretend to bite any of the dogs, regardless of their rank, and never worried about the consequences, and often she got her own way. She also exhibited both dominant and passive dominant traits, whereas other aspects of her behaviour defied both dominance and passive dominance theories.

FLY'S GUIDE TO PRACTICAL PARENTING

In the year 2000, Fly had her first litter of pups by Aled Owen's world champion Bob. Two weeks prior to giving birth, Fly ran at a sheep-dog trial at Ravensthorpe, Northamptonshire and worked well without being placed. The next day we travelled to another trial, at Drayton Parslow, near Milton Keynes. As always, Fly ran out quickly to gather her sheep, but on reaching them she lifted her head and ran back and refused to work. I was totally bemused, as was the judge, as she had never done this before or since.

The next day I took her to a farm in Willoughby Waterleys where I worked and exercised my dogs. Because they had had a busy weekend trialling, I walked them to the fishing pond where they could have a swim, and they all ran off on the command 'in the water'.

No teeth, but the message is clear.

Usually they would jump or squeeze under or through the gate into the pond area, but on this occasion when Fly reached the gate she stopped and waited. Normally she would have squeezed under the gate and made her own way into the field. When I reached the gate I encouraged her to go under it, but she stood firm and resolute, and I had little option but to open it for her, upon which she made her way to the pond. She had quite obviously decided that because she was heavily pregnant it was time to look after herself.

Two weeks later she produced a litter of seven

puppies, and her behaviour towards visitors changed instantly, even with those she knew very well, although she did not change in her attitude towards family members. She was immensely over-protective of her puppies, and if she felt anyone were threatening them would instinctively lunge forwards to snap at their face. As a mum, she could not be faulted in any way. Right from the very start she was happy to leave them, sometimes for quite a long time, but the pups never went hungry.

But when the pups were six weeks old, I made the mistake of feeding Fly in her whelping bed while the pups slept. One pup awoke and made its way towards her whilst she was eating, and she instantly and instinctively attacked it, without prior consideration, thought, or warning. It died shortly after. This pup had stood out from the litter from birth, and had whined and whimpered excessively, although it was always the smartest of them all at finding the rear and fullest teats. I had considered there might have been something wrong with it, but obviously was never to find out.

As the pups' eyes opened and they began to develop, Fly played a full role in educating them, in a very forthright and matter-of-fact manner. She was tough yet gentle, and continued to let them suckle as long as they wanted until she could no longer put up with the pain of sore nipples. Then she would let them know they had to stop in no uncertain terms with a growl, or by placing her teeth gently round their necks, applying just enough pressure to make a point.

MY INTRODUCTION TO PHOBIAS

Having reared her pups in my kennels at the top of the garden, I wanted Fly to stay up there once the pups were sold. She, however, had other ideas. During bonfire night and many times thereafter she chewed through her kennel wall and squeezed through a chain-link fence to return to what she considered to be the safety of the utility room. Having stopped this by reinforcing the chain link, she then chewed through a 3 × 2in fence post to escape. Next I placed her in a cage, thinking this was for her own safety, but returned home to find that once again she

Practical parenting – Fly shows her gentler side.

Swaledale ewes on the Caudals estate, the Langtons.

had chewed through the metal and escaped; her mouth bleeding and sore from her efforts to escape to freedom. I decided to leave her loose in the top half of the garden, and once more she chewed a hole in a brand-new trellis in order to find sanctuary near the house.

During fireworks or thunderstorms Fly strongly resisted any commands to go to the top of the garden. On quiet days she would happily walk to the top of the garden, but as soon as she saw me moving towards the kennels, she would turn and run off, and calls or commands asking her to come to me fell on deaf ears. It became

normal to find her in her cage under the work-top in the utility room, which was dark and where she obviously felt secure. A simple change of direction or a particular way of look-ing at her was enough to send her running in the opposite direction to hide; even accidental behaviour such as treading on her feet could result in her instantly and instinctively growling and pretending to bite the culprit on the feet, though she never followed it through to a seri-ous attack.

My kennels are now reinforced with chequered plate metal. However, I conceded

her moments. The door and plaster wall nearest to the kitchen door are reinforced with chequered plate, and when she senses a thunderstorm, she scratches on the door to come in and is allowed to do so. In her old age her hearing has faded and she is less disturbed by fireworks. Although some of Fly's antics have caused a great deal of trouble and consternation, she has nevertheless been a fabulous dog to own, and is dearly loved by everyone in the family.

FLY AS A TRIALS DOG

As regards sheepdog trials, Fly won her first ever nursery trial at Colin Pickford's farm at Rainow in Macclesfield in 1998. Ironically Colin finally handed me an envelope with the prize money in 2006, containing a crumpled £5 note. She also went on to win the Nursery Championship at Hayfield in 1998. She was remarkably easy to run, and required very little training to be able to run at trials. And when I started training her in 2002 on the Caudal hill in Leicestershire, she excelled beyond compare: this was obviously where she had found her niche. Despite her early weakness she was helpful around the farm, and even her shedding and penning improved markedly with age, as did her power. She was a line dog, and rarely needed a flank command. She balanced exceptionally well, and tucked in any wayward ewe without excessive use of her body, and without my having to command her. Her free-moving style on well chosen courses and sheep made her an easy and most reliable dog to run.

defeat and moved Fly back closer to the house, into the utility room. Here she was happy until sensing a thunderstorm she once more scratched the kitchen door until her nails were worn right down and her feet cut and torn. Having once again reinforced the door with chequered plate, in the run-up to bonfire night the following year she scratched and chewed the plaster round the door frame, leaving a gaping hole in the wall.

Now aged thirteen years old, Fly appears to have at last settled down and seems resigned to growing old gracefully, though she still has

However, as much as she improved, she was not my type of dog for trialling, largely because her slow and wide flanks frustrated me. Because I had got Spot and Skerry, both out of Fly, I rarely ran her at trials – but when I did run her in open trials, she was normally in the money or not far off it, despite my not specifically training her for competition.

The Passive Resistance Legacy

Fly produced three litters with some nineteen puppies, and passive resistance was prevalent in all, but in a relatively minor form. All the owners were pre-warned and only one dog has been re-homed, to my knowledge, for refusing to compete in agility. He now works sheep on Gwyn's farm, and elements of passive resistance are still extremely obvious. Sometimes even experienced handlers struggle to come to terms with this type of behaviour, yet in many cases when they are fully understood these dogs become the most tremendous pets and working animals, winning in competitions in a variety of disciplines.

DEVELOPING THE THEORY OF PASSIVE RESISTANCE

With no explanation of Fly's type of behaviour to be found in the various books I had about dogs and dog behaviour, I became fascinated with the traits that she was exhibiting. Over a period of time I began to notice that some elements of her behaviour were being evidenced by dogs both at my dog club and on the farm during sheepdog training sessions, though in a less aggressive way. In some cases it became clear that what we were observing was 'level one', or the early stages of the behaviour that we had witnessed with Fly. This enabled me to predict with relative accuracy the type of problems owners would have with their dogs, and sometimes whether the dogs would exhibit aggression towards members of the family. What was all the more important was the fact that I became confident of being able to resolve or manage the problems to a satisfactory outcome.

Some of the common traits observed were as follows:

- Refusal or resistance to getting off the settee or bed, or hiding under a desk or table.
- Fear- or phobia-based resistance to, or avoidance of thunderstorms, fans, fireworks, slippery floors, traffic, car chasing, doorways, cars, people, grooming brushes.
- Aggression in relation to food guarding or door guarding (leading to a privileged position).
- Refusal to move out of the way, or being stubborn.
- Refusal to go out of the house for walks or for toileting.
- Refusal to go into a kennel.
- Tolerance of high levels of pain if something were to be gained, such as food, freedom or safety.
- Hypersensitivity to sound, music, television programmes or telephones.
- Exaggerated shrieking or yelping to signify pain, often before pain is actually inflicted by another dog. This signifies a low pain threshold, either to prevent harm, warn others or as a means of ensuring or earning a privilege, such as entry into the house (*see below*).
- Deflection – creating opportunities – whereby a dog will distract another pack member either by sniffing a particular object or by giving out signals of becoming aroused or alert to something. This act will draw another dog away from a bone or privileged place in the kennel, such as the warmest place. I have also known dogs when put under pressure whilst training to suddenly develop a scratch that desperately needs to be dealt with: in doing so pressure is relieved, if only for a few seconds.

The following are some of the traits specific to Border Collies:

- Sensitive hearing – howling in reaction to the sound of the television, phones, church bells.
- They have a strong eye with the ability to 'tame' sheep.

- They are stronger and quicker with cattle.
- They have a high pain threshold.
- Bitches are protective towards their litter of pups.
- They refuse to work, or avoid working with another dog.
- They are sensitive to a raised voice or shouting whilst working.

The Calculated Approach

When littermates are playing with one another they will often shriek and squeal to signify when the others have caused them pain. This serves to check the behaviour of over-exuberant puppies whilst they are engaged in rough-and-tumble play, which can sound quite ferocious. However, I have observed passive resistant dogs take this behaviour a step further, using the same 'shrieking or yelping' to good effect to ensure no harm comes to them. They also use it as a self-defence mechanism to alert higher-ranking members of the pack that they are in trouble.

Over the years I had often heard Fly cry out loudly in the garden as though she were hurt, and normally Spot would be standing nearby looking sheepish. Although I always had my suspicions about anything Fly did, I had no evidence. However, on one occasion when I heard her screaming in the garden, I ran upstairs unnoticed and spied out of the window. The weather was turning and there was thunder in the air. For a while nothing happened, but then Fly let out an almighty scream, causing Spot to run up to her. He hadn't touched her or even looked at her, as far as I could see, yet Fly had orchestrated a situation, which on many previous occasions had led me not only to chastise Spot, but to let Fly into the house.

From that moment on I learned to ignore Fly. However, she then took the matter a step further. Whenever she sensed any atmospheric changes, such as a storm, and wanted to come into the house she would run and crash into the cage where Spot would be lying, minding his own business. This would provoke a reaction from Spot, who values his personal space, and cause a huge tussle between the two, inside the cage. Of course blood was never drawn, at least while I was around. Nevertheless, because I was now aware that Fly was manipulating me, I changed my stance and would either let Spot into the house, or would place both inside the cage and shut them in together. They were so shocked at this change in tactics that both would lie in there quietly and utter no sound at all!

Avoidance

Dogs in general can vary as to how many of the above traits they have, and therefore some dogs are easier to deal with than others. Needless to say, those dogs that are the most challenging have more passive resistance traits than those that have only one or just a few. In many cases the dog's refusal of, resistance to, or total avoidance of certain situations had an underlying cause such as fear or phobia of an object and/or a certain situation. Furthermore the refusal was not always a reaction to pressure from the handler, or a specific request.

However, a dog's refusal to do something almost always invokes a negative reaction from its owners, and as a result of this many passive resistant dogs I have worked with (some with behaviour problems) have developed a tendency to hide under a table, chair, under or inside a car or, in the absence of these, even behind their owner, in the vain hope that they cannot be seen or interacted with. They also avoid all eye contact. Building up trust with these dogs is crucial, and in severe cases where the dog is truly petrified, turning my back on it and avoiding eye contact altogether has borne fruitful results. Quite often the dog itself makes the first move, by sniffing or smelling me, by moving its nose closer to me, or choosing itself to make eye contact with me. Even where the causal link to particular objects or situations has not always been obvious, there is still a strong chance that these objects have become associated with a bad experience or trauma.

I have found it easier to achieve success if I work with the dog initially, rather than with the owners, as I am not emotionally attached to the dog. In some cases I have asked the owners to leave the room if they are projecting themselves as being very nervous and anxious. In a working situation I have asked to work with the dog whilst the owner looks on from a distance – where passive resistant dogs are concerned, a problem shared is a problem doubled! Some owners behave as if they, too, have the same fears and phobias as their dogs. Sometimes as a parent or dog owner you have to be prepared to administer 'tough love', in that feeling sorry for the dog can make the problem worse, and also risks making the dog more unstable.

I have observed many dogs refusing to work sheep, with their owners encouraging and giving false praise in order to persuade their young dog to work, but in vain. When a dog is not sure it will lie down and refuse to work, or may run away, or may stay close to its owner for comfort. In such cases greater force is called for, with firm commands. Dogs need to be discouraged from running back to their owner, and should be placed under greater pressure to run in the opposite direction. They need help to confront their fears, and should be placed inside the training pen and helped to make progress. Many owners are uncomfortable with this, and need a lot of persuading, but once the dog makes even a small breakthrough, further success will surely follow for both handler and dog.

Fortunately, dogs do not live in the past as we do. 'The most important thing to know about animals is that they all live in the present, all the time. It is not that they don't have memories – they do. It's just that they don't obsess over the past, or the future.' (Millan 2009, p. 199.)

It is of paramount importance that owners demonstrate a great deal of trust and faith in me, and strongly believe that their dogs will overcome the hurdles. It is also essential for me to remain calm, focused and free of emotion, and to trust in my judgement wholly. Once people observe that a more forceful approach actually instils greater confidence in their dogs, they are quite happy to proceed in this manner.

ALLEVIATING PASSIVE RESISTANCE PROBLEMS

Once a problem that is fear based or otherwise has been identified, it is essential that the situation is recreated many times so that you can practise and alleviate the problem. Don't just wait for the situation to occur again naturally, because almost certainly you will not be in the right frame of mind to tackle the problem. It is better to rehearse something thirty times a day, rather than wait for the dog to make that mistake thirty times and deal with it as it occurs. Sometimes you also need to decide whether it might actually be better to leave a problem alone and just give your dog time – but whichever path you choose you must be confident and positive about the outcome.

Cesar Millan in his *Dog Whisperer* programme has suggested many times over that no matter how positive or calm-assertive a person is, feelings of negativity such as anger, anxiety, frustration are so strong they can bring down even the cheeriest (Millan 2009, p. 206).

ALTERNATIVE MODEL OF PASSIVE RESISTANCE

In his book *Let the Dog Decide* Dale Stavroff also refers to the 'passive resister' (Stavroff 2007, p. 191) as having three traits:

- Whine or cry out in pain at the slightest provocation.
- Urinate submissively, or run and hide at raised voices, and go to their handler by crawling on their stomach.
- Freeze on the spot, when pressured by requests, sometimes drooling at the mouth for effect.

The model of 'passive resistance' offered by Dale Stavroff offers only tenuous links to the behaviour and traits I have described, and also suggests that 'passive resisters' display not some, but all of the three traits he mentions. He also suggests only to comfort the dog when it shows signs of distress *if it has been hurt* – and depending on the cause of the accident, any form of reassurance or reinforcement can potentially cause a conditioned response in the dog, which when faced with particular stimuli can induce fear.

BANDURA'S MODEL OF SELF EFFICACY AND OUTCOME

My theory of passive resistance has strong links with phobias and fear-based responses, and has more in common with Bandura's 'self efficacy, outcome and expectation' model of human behaviour conceived in 1977. Bandura received his PhD in Clinical Psychology in 1952 from the University of Iowa, and began teaching at Stamford University in 1953. In 2004 he was recognized for his 'Outstanding Lifetime Contribution to Psychology by the American Psychological Association'. Bandura's work is considered part of the cognitive revolution in psychology that began in the late 1960s, and his theories have had a tremendous impact on personality psychology, cognitive psychology, education and therapy (Wagner 2009).

Bandura suggested that humans were not driven exclusively by environmental factors (Wood and Bandura, 1989), and insists that behaviour is affected by both external (environmental) events and internal (cognitive) factors. (*See* Bandura, A. in References.)

Much of Bandura's research was devoted to understanding phobias, which typically result from the endless cycle of failure and self doubt, and he put forward three models in dealing with phobias or problems associated with self efficacy:

Vicarious experience: Characterized by a tendency for individuals to learn by watching others perform, and/or performing with others.

Verbal persuasion: Used to enhance performance and build self efficacy through guided encouragement. Verbal persuasion is effective in increasing self efficacy and changing behaviour only when the individual is truly capable of performing the behaviour.

Emotional arousal: Typically associated with emotions such as anxiety and fear, emotional arousal is one of the major obstacles in behavioural change as it reproduces a condition known as 'avoidance behaviour'.

On many occasions I have observed experienced sheepdog trainers using similar principles to those advocated by Bandura's model to resolve issues with dogs that were proving difficult to train. Young dogs can find it immensely difficult to get going on sheep, to outrun, drive sheep away, run out of sight and so on. I have also had older dogs come to me for training whose working instincts have been suppressed, and when their owner has let them off the lead they simply lie by the pen and watch the sheep, or follow the owner close by. They are often lacking in self belief, and the introduction of an older, experienced and calmer dog can tease out small threads of working instinct and give rise to a new level of confidence. This also serves to deflect any negative thoughts a young dog might have, which are preventing it from running after or chasing the sheep. Initially it might just run after the other dog, but gradually it will break away on its own and become more independent.

Bandura's model of vicarious experience is similar to what Cesar Millan refers to as the 'power of the pack'. Cesar uses his own dogs that are of stable mind to heal and rehabilitate not only aggressive dogs, but dogs that have experienced severe trauma and anxiety in their lives – for instance following an earthquake or accident.

Regarding the 'power of the pack', Cesar maintains that 'a dog's pack is his life force'. Instability within the pack, or a threat to it, affects each of its members, therefore 'the need to keep the pack stable and running smoothly is a powerful motivating force in every dog...

Why? It is deeply ingrained in his brain.' (*See* Millan, p. 111.)

It must always be borne in mind that for any healing to take place the mind must heal first, and only then will the physical behaviour follow. This can take time and patience. It is, however, crucial to any success that, even if the dog is failing in a work environment, it is nevertheless exercised and given the opportunity to offload some of the mental baggage it is carrying. This will ensure that it does not have nearly as much energy to feed the demons in its head. The same is true for people, in that the more time and energy we devote to thinking about a problem, the harder it becomes to face it and to remain positive: sometimes it is far better not to think or to analyse the problem, but to tackle it head on.

Working with an older dog can give confidence to a novice.

Case Study – Bob and Trim

In March 2009, Bob brought a two-year-old bitch, Trim, for sheepdog training. He had obtained this dog from a rescue centre, with a view to training it to work his flock of 'easy-care' sheep (a Welsh Mountain ewe crossed with a Wiltshire Horn ram). Trim had been partly trained and was supposed to know her sides, but Bob explained to me that, despite her previous training, Trim wasn't taking any commands from him and would not lie down.

As soon as he took her off her lead, she clapped (a dog that frequently drops to the ground) to the floor and eyed the sheep up and there she stayed, despite my moving the sheep and generally chasing them round the pen. Any command Bob gave her was in vain. In the excitement, three of the Hebridean sheep jumped out of the pen and Trim instantly set off after them. Bob set off after her, but I stopped him and asked him to hold firm and leave Trim to her own devices, trusting in the fact that if she knew her sides she would be armed with a reasonable degree of competence.

Having waited for a good minute we then caught sight of the three ewes returning, with Trim in close pursuit. She had snapped out of her earlier spell and was quite insistent in wanting to continue, as she held the sheep to me. A minute or so later I blocked her way to the sheep without giving a command, placed her on a lead, and Bob took her back to the pen.

I worked Skye for a little while as Trim looked on; this time she was alert and on her feet, ready to have a go. Bob took her off the lead and walked into the pen. I advised him to stay silent and move the sheep around the pen. Each time he moved the sheep, Trim covered them in both directions and when the sheep came to a stand still Trim willingly took the 'down' command from Bob. Within five minutes Trim was working in the pen, keeping a good distance from the sheep and taking the 'down' command from Bob. It would have been easy to have labelled Trim as a 'clapper' and to have stopped her from running after the sheep, yet that was the turning point, which brought her out of her shell. Sometimes by holding off from making any corrections, what develops is a whole lot more natural, with the progress being sustained.

(Information courtesy Robert Willington.)

There is still very little written on the subject of passive resistance, yet I have found this concept to be one of most significant when trying to understand difficult or problem behaviour. I have observed behaviour practitioners struggle to come to terms with aspects of passive resistant behaviour, and give up trying to resolve the issues. In some of these cases the solution was not only within easy reach but easy to achieve, in a relatively short time span. Yet they are repeatedly persuaded by the dog to give up and concede defeat.

I recall watching one of the many television behaviourists working with a Border Collie puppy that had developed a tendency to freeze and come to a halt every time it reached a squeaky farm gate. The trainer took the dog for a walk and, true to form, the dog resisted at the same place as always. The trainer pulled the dog, giving a long lead, but each tug was met with a counter tug in the opposite direction. The more the trainer tugged the more the dog became empowered to stay put until the trainer conceded that he could not effect change:

- First, pulling on the lead and not being able to effect change was a simple matter of dominance. The trainer tugged, without success and the dog's refusal was reinforced, as was the fact that it was not only physically stronger, but also mentally stronger than the trainer.
- Second, the trainer should have known the outcome of his actions, well before he attempted any techniques to counter the dog's stubbornness and resistance. Had he not been 100 per cent sure of achieving success, it would then have been better to have left the dog well alone.
- Third, it was highly likely that the cause of the passive resistance in the dog was triggered by the squeak in the gate, and the trainer's ineffectiveness merely reinforced the fear or phobia. It is highly likely that next time the dog's resolve in resisting would have been far greater.

Although the above example does not directly relate to sheep work, the behaviour described and the controls put in place are very similar to those applied during training with sheep. During both work and at sheepdog trials there is a great possibility of phobia-related problems occurring: fear of sheep, crooks, handlers letting sheep out, people, traffic and so on.

There is little doubt that anyone wanting a dog specifically for work will choose a confident, outgoing pup in order to avoid problems of fear, sensitivity and lack of confidence. This was born out only recently when I informed several triallists in North Wales about Gwyn having a litter of very well bred pups for sale. Despite showing polite interest, at best, no one wanted a pup. Then at a sheepdog trial near Bala, Gwyn happened to bring one of the pups, aged ten weeks old. The pup was bold, confident on the lead, and outgoing, and invited offers from two triallists without any questions as to the pedigree, eye test or otherwise. Unfortunately

Gwyn had chosen this pup for himself and she was no longer for sale.

Despite there being many issues presented by passive resistant dogs, ranging from mild to severe, the vast majority of the dogs bond well with their human counterparts. The common factor in all these cases is that the owners had no choice but to change and learn a new way of working through the problems. In extreme cases, passive resistant dogs exhibit aggressive and threatening behaviour; in mild cases, the behaviour can be totally eradicated; and in the worst case scenarios, I educate the owners to avoid the aggression.

I have observed an increase in the occurrence of passive resistant behaviour over the past ten years in both Border Collies and other breeds. The more probable scenario, however, is that it is not the numbers that have increased, but rather I have developed a better understanding of the traits displayed by passive resistant dogs and have recognized its features more easily.

One might think that animals acting out a phobia or fear of something might visibly display signs of anxiety; however, in some cases they have appeared perfectly calm. Perhaps this is because they have not only locked out their limbs to avoid being physically pushed closer towards the source of their fear, but possibly their minds also – rather like a child that doesn't want to hear something and proceeds to cover their ears and hum, to block out any sound. Perhaps the aim of locking out is that if they remain quiet and still, their actions will somehow persuade us to reconsider our plans.

I recall my dog Skerry behaving in this way. Sometimes, on arriving at the farm, I would let the dogs out on to the track and they would run, either next to the car, in front or behind. During certain times of the year I would look in my car mirror to check on the dogs and see Skerry standing thirty to forty metres away, perfectly still, looking towards the car. She did not hide or run away, although I felt that was more through

The mere mention of water, and Skerry would do anything for you.

my calm reactions to her behaviour than chance. I had learned not to put added pressure on her when I observed her in such a state. I didn't rule out her being pre-oestrus or pre-seasonal, as this behaviour did not occur regularly, sometimes two to three months prior to her coming into season. I would simply get out of the car and, being careful not to raise my voice, call her in a soft, normal voice. She generally came straightaway, and I would then follow up with a work-related command such as 'Away' or 'Come bye', which was generally enough to get her to run ahead of the car, with the other dogs.

Even in other situations, where dogs hide under a car or table or in some dark corner, they look perfectly calm and still. Of course, from a dominance perspective, this behaviour might have served as a submissive gesture, although I would have thought that a dog that was put under pressure might have rolled over in submission, as a passive dominant gesture. Also I would have expected dogs to be shaking or drooling out of fright, but this is never the case; instead they demonstrate great control and resilience even when faced with fearful situations.

ASSESSING PASSIVE RESISTANCE

Passive resistance can be observed in dogs of all

ages; however, what is difficult, particularly when you are faced with a young puppy, is to determine the extent to which it is passive resistance. I believe all dogs are passive resistant to some extent, just as all dogs have dominant and passive dominant tendencies. The major difference is that the two forms of dominance can be dealt with successfully as the puppy grows older, but puppies with a large number of passive resistant traits will remain this way for life. What will be different is the ability of the handler to learn to manage their own responses to passive resistance behaviour from their puppy.

In some older dogs of eight years and older I have observed aggression and stronger tendencies towards refusal to occur. Differences have also been observed when bitches are in or close to their season, pregnant, or nursing a litter. They exhibit an innate desire to guard food, or they are highly motivated by food, based on the primitive need to ensure survival of their puppies.

As far as the pack is concerned, as existing members get older and younger and stronger members join the pack, an older, more dominant dog will begin to lose its dominance/pack leader status or status within the pack. However, when it comes to dogs that are passive resistant, they may well appear to give up their status or ranking. However, in certain situations – for example, if they find a source of food first – they will stand their ground and be prepared to fight for the food rather than give it up to the higher ranking animal. This is why greater thought and planning is called for when dealing with passive resistant dogs, as they do not back down at the first sign of threat or aggression. You have to learn to 'box clever' with these types of dog.

It is also worth remembering that a bitch may temporarily gain a higher ranking position within a pack both before and during a season. Once the hormones settle down again she is then quite amiable and less resistant to moving back down the pack.

MANAGING PASSIVE RESISTANCE

In order to avoid a situation getting out of hand, or an older and lower ranking passive dog becoming aggressive, you have to learn to pinpoint the triggers and pre-empt the aggressive act taking place. Simply by giving a 'No' command at the right time, or indeed using the dog's name firmly, will ensure that they respect your authority and keep any aggressive undertones or thoughts in check. In short, make your intentions perfectly clear and set the guidelines from the very onset, in every situation, that may give advantage to a lower ranking dog. Silence on the handler's part in this type of situation will be perceived by your dog as a licence for him or her to assert their authority towards lower or higher ranking dogs. Food can be the source of many incidents of aggression, and a less rigid feeding regime when puppies are still with their littermates may encourage a slightly more nonchalant attitude towards food. The downfall of this is that passive resistance only becomes prevalent – or rather, obvious – as the puppy develops. If you have evidence of food guarding, then it may well be worthwhile incorporating a free feeding regime, as mentioned above, for a limited time period.

Passive resistant dogs may also refuse to carry out instructions, such as going into a kennel or out of the house, or to leave sheep after work – they will stop working, but will lie down and refuse to come back to you; they might even run to a person nearby, or simply run off. My own Skye, when she was a year and a half old, was working some sheep at Flintham Show as part of a demonstration. Following a few minutes of work to demonstrate how a young dog starts working sheep, I called her to jump into the car. She came towards me, but then ran straight past and towards the main ring. There was no panic: I simply kept my calm and waited, and she returned without command. In many instances dogs may refuse to come to you because they have become conditioned to a particular command or mannerism. In Skye's case, finishing work and being asked to jump into the car acted as a trigger to predict my behaviour. This refusal remains the most frustrating aspect of her behaviour and is evident at every trial I attend.

If you find yourself in a similar situation, rather than becoming angry at your dog or shouting, when your dog starts to run off, try the following:

- First, give a stop command, either 'Stand' or 'Lie down'. I prefer the former, because it avoids the dog locking out.
- Once your dog has stopped, distract him/her either with a hand signal or by clicking your fingers or offering an exciting command such as one associated with work, such as 'Look back', then walk over to him. He will not run away unless you raise your voice or show anger.
- Once you have reached your dog, hold him/her gently by the collar and ask him to come with you, ensuring that you do not pull on the collar. If there is any tension on the collar he will drag his heels.

As an alternative to the above, where your dog's refusal or resistance is not based on fear, but sheer obstinacy, with a risk of your dog going to ground, then a slightly different approach can be taken. If, for example, you want your dog to leave a particular room or even farm building or kennel block and you are met with a refusal, then ignore the first refusal you get. Leaving the door open, go out without your dog, and pause for a few seconds. Then use a word that you know has a predictably conditioned response to

excitement, or pretend to talk to another dog using this word, and your dog will soon come to investigate what you are up to. One of my favourites is 'Dinner time!'.

At sheepdog trials, after exercising my dogs, when it is time for the dogs to return to the car, Spot, my oldest dog, is always last to get to the car, normally finding something to smell just at the time I would normally call him. Rather than call him and be met with a refusal, I would time my command to perfection and call out 'Dinner time!' and walk out of sight. As soon as I moved I would normally find Spot with me. Occasionally I would introduce a food reward, ask him to jump into the car, and then offer it. Other excitement commands can be working commands such as 'Look back' or even 'Look'. At other times I take out a crook from the back of my car and no sooner have I done this, than Spot is standing next to me, thinking we are about to run in the trial.

By acting in this way you are not pandering to your dog, and you most certainly are not losing face: you are applying dog psychology and out-thinking your dog.

PASSIVE RESISTANCE IN PARTICULAR BREEDS

I have observed passive resistance in many breeds of dog other than Border Collies, such as the Rough Collie, the Irish Setter, the Italian Spinone, the Weimeraner, the English Bulldog, the Miniature Bull Terrier and the Bull Terrier, the Springer Spaniel, and Whippet as well as cross-bred dogs. I do not believe, however, that these particular breeds produce passive resistant dogs per se. I also have no evidence to suggest that there are more passive resistant dogs than dominant dogs in particular breeds, and feel that greater research is necessary in this area.

Regarding Border Collies, however, I have observed certain traits as being common to dogs that are passive resistant, and occasionally these traits are also shared by passive resistant dogs from other breeds. As mentioned earlier, Fly has produced nineteen puppies, and their owners have reported elements of passive resistance in all of them. In addition, many have also reported that the puppies have sensitive hearing and have been known to howl at church bells, telephones, music, television programmes and so on. Many of the puppies that have gone to working homes have also shown a certain degree of eye, which has been particularly prevalent when lifting sheep. Once again, although the puppies did share a number of common traits, there was also a marked variance in them. For example, my own Mac howls to church bells but is tolerant of music and the television, whereas Spot becomes very agitated and howls uncontrollably at the quietest of music, yet is fine with church bells.

I have also observed that passive resistant dogs are sensitive to unfair pressure, shouting, frequent commanding and heavy handedness, and also have a fear of fireworks, gunfire and thunderstorms. Where the dogs have been sensitive, they have been less so in a working environment, and so a degree of pressure has still been necessary to overcome some issues.

DOES PASSIVE RESISTANCE SERVE A PARTICULAR ROLE?

The examples of passive resistant behaviour described in this chapter clearly point to the fact that when a dog refuses or resists particular demands, it does so because it feels under threat or disadvantaged in some way. In some cases, our demands place them under threat or pressure, and cause them anxiety, stress and ultimately fear; in other instances some passive acts may also serve ultimately to give advantage or bring reward to the dog. There is no logic or thought that goes into their decision making, and their refusal is not premeditated: they make an informed, snap decision based on that moment, and block any attempts to persuade them otherwise. Also the factors that induce anxiety may have inadvertently become associated with a past bad experience. Whatever the reason that causes a dog to act in the above manner, one thing is clear: the dog feels it has strong reasons for resisting. What can be a stronger, more motivating force than survival?

In 1932, Walter Cannon, an American psychologist, coined the phrase 'fight or flight', which is a response that occurs when animals are faced with danger (*see* Seaward, 2005). This response to acute stress causes a change in the sympathetic nervous system and prepares animals to either run away or stay and fight. A third response was also put forward by psychologists whereby an animal freezes, panics or passes out, rather than fleeing or fighting. This is commonly seen when a deer 'freezes' in the headlights of an oncoming car, or a sheep collapses when chased by a dog.

Whatever the reason behind passive resistance, I remain confident that dogs will continue to behave in such a manner for hundreds of years more, and that trainers and handlers will either have to risk losing good working dogs, or acquire the knowledge to work them and adapt their handling style. I strongly believe that as much as I hated Fly's working style, namely her eye and laid-back approach, what she has passed on to her progeny has been priceless, namely the ability to get close to sheep without inducing fear or panic.

The habit of winning comes from sacrifice and single-mindedness. To want something so much but to have the presence of mind to wait and be patient, and to execute a plan without emotion or being hindered by past events, perfectly depicts a dog's mind.

Portrait of a Successful Handler – Jim Cropper

Jim Cropper describes in his own words what it takes to become a successful handler, and the type of dogs that make successful sheepdogs.

As a young lad of ten I lived in a terraced house between Rawtenstall and Burnley in Lancashire. Over the road was a farm I used to visit and watch a Border Collie called Lassie work the sheep. I must have been greatly influenced by the dog because I asked my father if I could buy one. Eventually after months of pestering I got one from a local farmer with no particular breeding; I also called it Lassie. Not very successfully, the dog would try to round up chickens.

It was years later that I took more interest in sheepdog trialling and once I started running dogs my main influence was Tot Longton. We travelled miles together going to many trials. Tot was a great sheep man and had the enviable ability to pen the wildest sheep. Although he never offered specific advice to me there was nevertheless a lot I picked up from listening to him. He commented on other handlers' runs and how the sheep were behaving.

Another handler I was influenced by was Jock Richardson from Peebles, in Scotland. One of the most memorable runs I ever saw was at the International at Cardiff, when he won the Supreme Champion title with Wiston Cap (31151). Cap had gears like a Rolls Royce, and he also had superb brakes. I learned a lot from watching Jock and other top handlers. Perhaps the most valuable lesson I learned was to watch the sheep and not the dog. You could say I was self taught, as I listened and took note of the top handlers and studied them very carefully.

Our land at Bacup, in Lancashire, where Shirley and I farm, consists of rough terrain: large hills, deep gullies, rough bent blow grass and boggy areas. This type of land is helpful to train a dog to look and guide them to sheep, whistling them in and out.

The dogs I like must be spirited and keen to give me something to work on. I prefer dogs with stamina that are long legged and smooth coated. I also prefer to run dogs as opposed to bitches as they cope better with pressure from strong handling and I don't have seasons to contend with!

To become successful I have spent a lifetime studying sheep and dogs. When I go to a trial I study the sheep and the course, even though I talk to plenty of folk. It is also essential to have good reflexes and vision. People sometimes ask me how I manage to appear so calm when running dogs. I may appear to be calm, but nerves are there. I don't show them, as dogs can get nervous. I also believe in making your own luck by working hard.

(Information courtesy of Jim Cropper.)

Jim Cropper – the calmest of all handlers I have seen.

CHAPTER 5

HOW DOGS THINK

SINGLE MINDEDNESS

Dogs think in a manner that is very single minded. They remain eternally optimistic and do not engage in pessimistic thinking or worrying – for example, where the next meal will come from. And always bear in mind that whether you breed your own dogs or buy them from a sheepdog sale, their allegiance will be exactly the same: to themselves. They will not care one iota that you might have paid £2,000 for them, and that you will be expecting great things from them on the farm or trial field. They will, however, expect things from you.

There is a great misconception amongst many dog owners that their working dogs or pets love them unconditionally. Yes, your dogs might not care whether you remember their birthday, and they won't sulk if you don't buy them a Christmas present or pay them a compliment now and again. However, they do have expectations. They will expect you to provide food, exercise and – last but not least – a means of living within a social context as part of a pack. It is ironic that the need to exercise stems from the hunting instinct, and despite the fact that dogs have been domesticated for hundreds of years, and that their human leaders have taken on the role of food provider, exercise remains high on their list of priorities.

Those dogs that are pure in their breeding – those that are very close relatives of the wolf –

provide the greatest challenge to handlers. Their instincts are to ensure survival, and they are highly motivated by food and exercise – or to put it another way, hunting. These types of dog are highly predatory, and exhibit aspects of such behaviour during training. Of course they will be grateful that you provide them with a daily meal, but should the opportunity present itself for a little extra, your dog will see no justifiable reason why it shouldn't help itself to that little extra, as instinct takes over – to grip a ewe, for example.

How many times have you seen a young dog do a great outrun, only to come in tight at the end and grip a ewe? From your dog's perspective, he is trying to bring the food back to you in the quickest possible manner – and how can you expect to control the instinct to kill in a few months of training when this very same instinct has survived generations, over hundreds of years of human interference, through breeding practices? Exercise remains a primary need in dogs. Provide this, and they will be less likely to use their energy to challenge you. (The same is strangely true for children.)

The way dogs think is fundamentally different to humans, with the exception of some professional sportsmen. Australians and Americans, in particular, grow up and are brought up with a winning mentality, to think positive even in difficult and adverse situations. They rise to a challenge and work well under pressure. They are not fazed by adversity, rather they relish it. It is a well known fact that American children, at a very early age, swear an allegiance to their national flag, whereas English children in primary schools are brought up to believe that 'it is the taking part that counts, not the winning'. Ironically the people preaching these ideals often do so from powerful, privileged positions, which they acquired through ignoring the very same advice they now find themselves offering.

Over the past fifty years (1959–2009) Wales has won the International Sheepdog Trials on twenty-one occasions and Scotland nineteen times. England meanwhile has only been successful on eight occasions, and Ireland twice (Ireland ran in the International for the first time in 1961). Of the eight handlers that were successful for England, one was of Welsh origin and two (both the same handler) were of Scottish origin (Main 1906–2006). Could this have anything to do with their strong national identity, pride and single mindedness as a race, or is it just coincidence? The last Englishman to win the coveted title was Sydney Price in 1987. On the face of it, both the Welsh and Scots appear to have a strong unified identity and are visibly proud of their national heritage and flag, whereas the English are less overt in any demonstration of national pride. Even where individuals have attempted to demonstrate their national pride, by flying either the Union Jack or the flag of St George, this has been quashed.

Guiding Principle

John Thomas said to me a few years ago: 'It's easy to smile when you're winning, but learning to smile when things are going wrong is harder' (Courtesy Mr J. R. Thomas). We should all learn to celebrate success, no matter who achieves it, and to be gracious in defeat.

Putting conjecture to one side, the more probable answer lies in the fact that Scottish and Welsh handlers have acquired and harnessed their skills on harsh hills and mountains. Working routinely against the elements with large numbers of sheep, the art of practical shepherding was forced on them, which for many handlers today is unattainable, given the economic climate.

When Should You Be Satisfied?

Whenever I ask the following question I almost always get the same answer: 'If in any given task you achieved one out of ten, would you be satisfied with this ratio?' In almost 100 per cent of cases the answer I am given by people is 'No'.

When a dog is faced with a situation whereby it only achieves one out of ten it does not react as humans do: feeling dejected, worthless, disappointed, a failure and so on. Dogs are happy with whatever they achieve, no matter how little it is. Whenever I eat a sandwich and drop a crumb on to the floor my dog Fly rushes to find it as though her life depended on it, and never looks disappointed with the amount. She merely tracks the floor and lifts her head looking to see if I might drop some more. What is also amazing is that even though the sandwich crumb is minute, her sense of smell is acute enough to find it.

Dogs will always be happy with whatever they achieve in the knowledge that a crumb is better than no crumb at all. Furthermore if one crumb is discovered, then there is always a possibility that two might be found, then three, four, and five and so on. Where a dog is concerned, success, even on a small scale, can always be built upon, and they remain ever the optimist. We should learn from our dogs by adopting this way of thinking when we train them on sheep. By expecting very little from them you will achieve success much more quickly, and you can use this as a sounding board and build from it. Moreover, dogs do not live in the past or the future: rather they live for the present, and this ensures they are not burdened, as humans are, with unnecessary baggage that interferes with their thoughts and expectations, and most importantly, how they perceive the world.

Given the above scenario, it strikes me that although people can be quite hard on themselves if they achieve below expectation, if a child achieves one out of ten in a given task, their parent would celebrate this and give encouragement. They would celebrate succeeding on one occasion rather than commiserate on failing in nine. So why is it that we do not afford ourselves the same leniency that we do our children? Surely most children grow up to be encouraged and to be satisfied with one out of ten? So when does the transition occur that causes people to become dissatisfied?

In the UK, children attend nursery and pre-school from four years old; by the time they reach seven years of age, there is greater emphasis on competition from parents and teachers. The children themselves become more competitive in their play. Children are expected to achieve school targets and attainment targets, and are thereby taken out of their comfort zone and faced with greater challenges.

It is not a case of having lower expectations: rather it is about being satisfied that some success is achieved, and believing that if it is possible to achieve a low level of success, then through perseverance and some luck it should be possible to build on that and achieve more.

Where puppies are concerned, the way in which they view the world and the successes they achieve is no different whether they are seven weeks old or seven years old. The only factors that change are their intensity and level of confidence.

I recall listening to an interview with John McEnroe, the former tennis player, during Wimbledon 2008. He was referring to a memorable final he had had against Bjorn Borg in 1980. John spoke at length about how well he had played, particularly in the first and fourth sets. When he had finished, the interviewer asked him who had won. John replied tentatively 'Bjorn', and changed the subject. Twenty-eight years after the final, McEnroe was still only picking out the positive aspects of his game, rather than dwelling on the negative aspects. (Incidentally the results were: 1-6, 7-5, 6-3, 6-7, 8-6 to Borg.)

A winner should never, ever be satisfied with his/her achievements, but he/she should also celebrate them, no matter how small. This is especially important to remember when training young dogs, to celebrate small levels of success and to take each stage slowly. Also feelings of dejection and disappointment can have a negative impact on future success. If things don't go to plan, move on and either accept you had bad luck or work harder.

Feodor Dostoevsky reputedly said that 'If everything on earth were rational, nothing would happen': in this respect many aspects of dog behaviour continue to baffle us although in the vast majority of cases the explanation is not quite so complex as one might imagine.

CHAPTER 6

THE IMPORTANCE OF SCENT TO DOGS

THE PREDOMINANCE OF THE SENSE OF SMELL

Even as a child, before I had dogs, I had heard of the saying 'dogs can sense fear'. However, where this quote came from has remained a mystery to me. It was only through the advent of the dog appeasement pheromone – better known as the DAP diffuser – at the beginning of the millennium that I began to acknowledge the importance of smell to dogs. Developed in France by scientists, the function of this pheromone was to provide safety, comfort and reassurance to dogs at times of stress and anxiety – and it became apparent to me that dogs don't just sense fear, they smell it.

It is well documented that animals use pheromones to communicate with one another, and it should always be borne in mind that we are a part of the animal kingdom. The basis of the theory behind DAP was the fact that puppies are born without the ability to see or hear; these senses develop a little later, at between seven to fourteen days, with the eyes being the first to open. However, puppies are born with the ability to smell, and for the first few minutes of their lives, and thereafter, they rely on their sense of smell to negotiate their way towards their mother's teats, thereby finding the source of milk. This contains colostrum, which is so crucial to the survival of puppies and other young animals.

It is believed that bitches nursing a litter periodically secrete a natural pheromone into the air, which serves to keep the puppies feeling safe and secure. Because scientists have been able to reproduce this pheromone, dog owners can now artificially recreate a feeling of calm during periods of stress or anxiety caused by fear of fireworks, travelling in cars and so on. If the sense of smell in puppies is acute enough to ensure their survival, then it is understandable that as they grow older they will continue to rely predominantly not on their sight, but on their sense of smell.

Both canine and human noses contain a bony scroll-shaped plate, called tubernates. When observed through a microscope this organ reveals a membrane containing scent detection cells and nerves. In humans this is about the size of a stamp when unfolded; in

---

Guiding Principle

It is only when we look beyond the embarrassment of our dogs greeting one another by smelling their anal glands or people's crotches, do we start to realize and accept the fact that whereas humans look at and assess the world with their eyes, dogs do so through their sense of smell.

Mac and Skye up to no good.

dogs the same membrane when unfolded would be the size of an A4 sheet of paper. This membrane varies in size from breed to breed, depending on the size of the snout. The proportion of a dog's brain devoted to analysing smells is forty times larger than that of a human, therefore it has been estimated that dogs can smell between 1,000–10,000 times better than humans (Stanley & Hodgson, 2007).

It is no wonder that dogs appear to react to situations unpredictably, or are aroused or frightened by situations for reasons which to us make no sense. This is because we cannot appreciate the source of their fear or anxiety.

What the Eye Cannot See!

I recall walking on the moors near Sheffield in the year 2000, when Spot and Skerry were six months old. As we walked up a small track we were flanked on either side by stone walls high enough to prevent me looking over them. Part

way on the walk I noticed Spot and Skerry becoming very excited; Spot tried to climb up one of the walls, but I stopped him. Curiosity got the better of me, however, and I, too, decided to have a look. Standing on tip toes I peaked over to find three Swaledale rams taking shelter from the sun about fifty metres or so away. I knew I was in for trouble if the dogs' sense of smell was as acute as this – and I was proved right, because back home, the pair would go looking for sheep when we were out for walks, and even if I took them to fields where there were no sheep, they would manage to find some by scenting.

The Smell of Confidence!

Sense of smell is extremely important to a dog when it is running on big courses in order to find sheep. Whenever you ask your dog to 'look' for sheep, look at their nose and you will observe its tip twitching as it uses its sense of smell to scent for them. Just as gundog trainers teach their dogs to find dummies hidden out of sight, it is a good idea to teach young dogs to find sheep by taking some fleece and getting them to scent for it. Later you can progress to finding actual sheep.

For many people if something can't be seen, then it cannot possibly exist, and this is the worst possible basis on which to start a relationship with their dog or puppy. Both pups and dogs can invoke, in humans, the most intense feeling of helplessness and frustration, not to mention anger, simply through their dogged determination and single-mindedness. If it is possible for nursing bitches to secrete pheromones in order to keep the pups feeling safe and secure, then I would hypothesize that every human emotion carries a specific smell or pheromone. This in turn would lead to a physiological change, such as a change in body temperature, which dogs might respond to. It is,

however, a matter of further research to determine whether a nursing bitch can secrete pheromones at will, rather than as a matter of unsolicited reaction.

'Right and wrong' are human concepts, and it is so easy for us to humanize situations. But I do believe that the answer is a whole lot simpler. Thus if we are angered by something that a dog does, it will smell our pheromones, as well as observe other visual and chemical signals associated with our emotion, and it will therefore become wary of us. In the same way, if we are happy, again our dogs will smell this and will be happy to share our company. Through experience dogs will come to understand our differing moods and resulting behaviour, and will develop a library of our various smells to then predict our behaviour. Further, as dogs become tuned to our various emotions it is then highly likely that our mood will be projected in how our dog behaves.

Evening on the Caudals – the work is done.

I have worked with many sheepdog handlers who, because they are new to training a dog on sheep, become confused and despondent, are hesitant and unsure as to which direction to move in or at what pace, when to walk towards sheep and when to walk away. This uncertainty has been mirrored in how their dogs have worked: running away, refusing to flank in a particular direction, sniffing, and eating grass and so on. In some cases any attempts by me to intervene have also been futile due to the nega-tive effect of the presence of the owner. Cesar Millan writes in his book *Be the Pack Leader*: 'If we are unsure about how we are feeling, or what energy we are projecting at any given moment, all we have to do is look to our dogs to figure it out' (Millan 2009, p. 199). The dog is like a large mood ring!

In a training situation when you are trying to introduce new and challenging concepts to young dogs, scent can play a tremendous part in determining how your dog works. Of course,

---

Case Study – Nathalie and Tess

Nathalie, one of my clients, had never before worked a dog on sheep, but following some inten-sive work we had managed to progress out of the training pen. Tess, her one-year-old bitch, was always extremely keen and impatient to get on with her work, and invariably this made life diffi-cult for Nathalie, because even before coming to the sheep, Tess pulled excessively on the lead to get to them. I always knew when they had arrived, because I could hear Nathalie commanding Tess to stop pulling, often in vain.

Following a three-week break from training I had once again booked a session with Nathalie and Tess. I decided that we would start in the training pen, so that Nathalie could refresh her mind about her positioning, without worrying about what the sheep were doing. She was greeted by five newly shorn Hebridean ewes waiting patiently and calmly in the centre of the pen. As usual Nathalie walked a short distance from the pen with Tess to start her off. However, as soon as Nathalie took the lead off, Tess escaped and made her way to the pen and beyond, where she waited at the point of balance, behind the sheep. Nathalie meanwhile made her way into the pen and proceeded to command Tess to flank to her right. Tess took every command and things were progressing rather well, despite her long break.

Then Nathalie decided to change to the left-hand flank, and despite repeated attempts and commands for Tess to flank to the left, she ignored Nathalie every time, for nearly five minutes. To make matters worse, she also refused to recall, thereby rendering Nathalie helpless. This was turning into a battle of wills and there was only ever going to be one winner: Tess. What made it particularly difficult for Nathalie was that there were observers present, so it was all the more important to her that Tess did not show her up. However, the more she tried, the more Tess was determined to get her own way. Tess did not care how many commands were given or how loud they were and took no notice of Nathalie's position or proximity. Nathalie even tried to apply pressure on her by running towards her, but this was in vain, as Tess was just that bit quicker. The sheep, meanwhile, surprisingly stood quite calm, rooted to the spot.

Nathalie was close to losing her voice when I asked her to stop working and have a break. Her voice had reached several different peaks and troughs, and served to fuel Tess rather than restrict her. She had also lost her temper; she sounded angry and frustrated and her despair was evident to all, her face now resigned to failure.

Following a short break Nathalie once again went inside the pen, but this time she was more composed. I asked her to remain calm and not to

owners can now make use of DAP diffusers, or similar products, to help with training or rehabilitating dogs. However, is there an alternative to buying this pheromone in a ready packaged form?

I always advise my clients that when you are calm you will *smell* calm and thereby inspire calmness. If, on the other hand, you are lively and excitable, your dog will smell the increase in adrenalin and become more predatory, with heightened senses ready for action. When dogs

use any commands whatsoever, either flanking or stop commands. I reminded her that whilst the sheep had stood still they served no purpose in determining which direction Tess ran in. Tess's futile running round the pen was caused by the fact that she was desperately trying to move the sheep. They, however, were quite content in the middle of the pen, grazing and glancing up now and again to see how she was progressing. This time Nathalie started with the left flank, but before doing so she first moved the sheep to Tess's left, causing her to run in the same direction. Once Tess had started to move I told Nathalie to continue moving in the same direction without stopping.

Tess naturally continued to run round and round until she began to tire. Then, just as she began to slow down, I asked Nathalie to double back and stop herself. Just as she got into position, Tess came to a sudden halt, stopping without a command. What is more important she took her eyes off the sheep and looked at Nathalie in acknowledgement. Nathalie was a whole lot happier, her voice now returned, and Tess was once again working in both directions correctly. Now that calm had been restored, Nathalie was able to work Tess out of the pen, and achieved the same level of control. The session ended on a good note for both handler and dog.

are wilful and intent on doing things their own way, if you just stop, and do not get involved in a confrontation with them, you will signal your intent and calm control, as well as your authority. It is all the more crucial that you develop the ability to think positively, to expect success and to remain assertive. When you are met with confrontation or adversity you must, above all, remain the model of calmness. By controlling and focusing your mind on positive outcomes you will not get drawn into negative territory and signal to your dog that they cannot effect change in your mental state. This will convey and signify strong leadership, which in turn will inspire confidence in young dogs, or older dogs lacking in confidence or sensitive and anxious dogs. There is no more potent force than the smell of confidence.

In order to focus one's mind, it is crucial to first stop any verbal communication. By remaining silent you are more likely to achieve a calm state than if you continue to speak. In the course of training, whenever you reach a point of conflict where your dog is either not achieving or not doing what it has been told to do, you need to ask yourself the question, 'How am I responsible for causing this situation?' In the majority of cases, your dog will make mistakes because you have made mistakes, and unfortunately it is a human flaw to deny any blame.

If the handler's attitude and mental preparation is right, then success is usually just round the corner. The line between success and failure is an extremely thin one, as is the line between your dog and the sheep. Crossing it can open up a gateway leading to a torrent of emotions and behaviours.

There is no dog more testing than the one which demonstrates sensitivity, and either runs off from the handler, goes to ground or runs back to the handler at times of uncertainty. Faced with such problems, can the handler dig deep, or should they consider an easier option, that of selling the dog or rehoming it?

CHAPTER 7

WORKING WITH NERVOUS OR SENSITIVE DOGS

ADMINISTERING TOUGH LOVE

It is extremely common to find that working dogs are nervous, anxious, sensitive and lacking in confidence. Most of my current clients' dogs are of this type, of which I would expect 90 per cent to become useful trialling dogs. Not everyone wants to win the National and or International, or even thinks that they can, and many are happy with turning out on Saturday afternoons and simply being able to have a complete run, or just having a useful dog on the farm.

It is a common fallacy to think that when you are faced with a dog that is sensitive or nervous you have to take a softer approach. The reasons why a dog may develop this type of character is usually due to failings in early socialization, or failure of the mother to nurture and spend time playing with the puppies. Some sensitive dogs may also have passive-resistant tendencies. Also if a bitch is bred from every season it will become ambivalent towards the litter, and the puppies will be neglected and fail to thrive. Whether human or animal, the world is a tough, cruel and sometimes harsh place. Many of us feel that we have to protect children or young animals from the pitfalls, but by doing so we are not doing them any favours because when faced with adversity in their daily lives, they may fail to cope, choosing instead to run away

from problems. Dogs may even run away from you, as might children.

Imagine a young child who loves to climb trees: is it not better that you teach that child how to climb safely, pointing out all the pitfalls and dangers? Alternatively, you could stop them from climbing altogether and risk that one day, when faced with a similar challenge, they will come to some harm because they were not aware of the dangers. I prefer the former.

If your dog is a nervous or sensitive type, you have to be confident and firm in how you work with that dog. However, being firm is not enough, and it is crucial that in all situations you must also be seen to be fair (see Chapter 9). You must be confident of your own actions, know how to tackle problems, when to tackle them, and when to leave well alone. Where dominance is concerned, a person or animal that is nervous will prefer the company of someone who knows their mind and inspires confidence. If you were lost in a forest with a child, you would not leave it to the child to take charge and lead you out: you would have to rise to the challenge, play the grown-up and take control. Even in our daily lives we look for partners who complement us and who can make up for our deficiencies.

Once your dog learns to trust in you as a leader, it will slowly but surely come to accept your training and subsequent commands, and will gain confidence in you.

Skerry had the talent but needed time and help to realize it.

SENSITIVE VERSUS CONFIDENT DOGS

Is being nervous or sensitive the same as having no confidence? Many people convey a negative meaning to the word 'sensitive', yet it means responsive, receptive, aware, and insightful, and I often wonder whether they are actually confusing their dog being sensitive with lacking in confidence, self-belief, faith and self-reliance. If this is indeed the case, then surely it is the role of the handler to have enough for both. Just as a good teacher can nurture the strengths of a shy young pupil and bring them out of their shell, a good handler can tease out their dog's strengths first before focusing on their weaker areas.

Many dogs are dismissed as either sensitive or lacking confidence, or as inadequate workers, but they blossom in later life and can then handle equally well the tasks that strong dogs would perform earlier with ease. It has perhaps been the case that the dog was armed all along with the necessary skills for the job, but was lacking in the self-belief to apply those skills. What some dogs need is time and a positive environment. They avoid sad or negative feelings

---

Guiding Principle

'Anger and intolerance are the enemies of correct understanding.'   Mahatma Gandhi

Case Study – David and Floss

When David phoned me about sheepdog training, he was quick to point out that Floss, his dog, was sensitive. It is only too easy to label a dog and to make assumptions about its level of sensitivity. A dog can be sensitive to particular objects, or to sounds such as gunfire, fireworks or even sudden rustling noises. Therefore it is more accurate to say that the dog has a tendency to be nervous when presented with certain situations, but it is not nervous in all situations, and without such stimuli it can present itself as perfectly 'normal'. Indeed we are the same, in that given a particular set of circumstances we are all capable of being over-sensitive, anxious, nervous and so on – but this does not mean that we should be categorized as such for the rest of our lives.

My first impressions of two-year-old Floss were that she was confident and outgoing, with a keen interest in sheep. Having not long arrived she ran confidently and positively on her outrun and overflanked the sheep, that were held in a round pen, by some two metres. She took firm commands, and despite David telling me that she didn't lie down easily, sometimes taking as many as six commands before she would do so, Floss proceeded to take every 'Down' command at the first or second time of being asked without being worried. What made the difference was the timing of the down command, in that she was more resistant to being asked to lie down behind the sheep, than she was when she overflanked them. As it was I preferred this option, because it ensured she covered all the sheep on her outrun.

Having allowed her to let off some steam we then moved away from the pen to send her on a left-hand outrun. She was not set up for the outrun in any way, and she lay facing the sheep square on.

David and I moved away from her by about seven metres so there was no pressure on her and she was given our full confidence. Due to her positioning it was easy to predict that her first movement would be wrong, so facing her square on I gave her a firm 'Down' command, and repeated this once more. On both occasions I observed that as I gave the command, she lowered her head, not as a sign of being afraid, but rather as a way of acknowledging she had understood.

David then took over. As he repeated the 'Down' command Floss's downward head movement was less pronounced until he gave a second, firmer command. Once again predicting that Floss would make a mistake at the onset, David gave her a 'Comebye' command when she turned her head slightly away from us, immediately followed by the 'Down' command, then again a second flank command was given, to initiate a perfect outrun.

Next David positioned Floss about three metres from the pen and asked her to flank past us. She failed to do this correctly, choosing instead to run in front of David – in fact she totally disregarded him, and it became clear that she did not totally regard herself and David as a partnership, and so lacked trust in him. We tried again, and this time stopped Floss before she reached the front of the pen. We repeated the process described above, at the start of the outrun and using the 'That'll do' command, followed by a flank command. This time Floss did flank on the far side of David, before continuing on her flank. Unfortunately at the point she passed David she was only a half a metre or so away from him, which would have unsighted her for a brief period.

In order to persuade Floss to maintain greater distance from David we needed either to stop and start the exercise, or to use some audible or visual stimulus to deflect her away from him. I chose to use a noise stimulus in the form of a carrier bag on a handle. However, before progressing, I knew that Floss would be quite sensitive to the bag, if not frightened, so I asked David to get her to lie down (fear is a barrier that can be broken down and overcome); then I brought the bag towards her, and despite not threatening her in any way, Floss moved away from it. I commanded her quite firmly to lie down, and then sat next to her, placing the bag next to her but avoiding all eye contact with her. For a while she fixated on the bag, but as she grew in confidence and relaxed, I then picked the bag up and put it down several times until she came to accept that neither the bag nor I intended her any harm. The problem was resolved, at least for now, because as I put the bag down she forced herself into my personal space and made a fuss of me.

We repeated the previous flanking exercise, but this time, at the point where Floss started to come in toward David's feet, I very gently and carefully banged the bag against my leg, causing her to move ten metres or so away from David and continuing on a beautiful flowing flank.

We had successfully used the source of Floss's fear to overcome a major fault, introducing the bag gently and desensitizing her so she was persuaded not to fear it, and then using it successfully to widen her flanks. It was not necessary to use the bag again. Floss was in no way distracted from her work, and never displayed the same level of fear she had shown at the introduction of the bag: she now associated it with working sheep, and enjoyed the fact that she was allowed to continue working, rather than the alternative method which would have caused her to stop and start, placing greater pressure on her.

(February 2009)

such as anger and frustration, so it is the owner's role to provide training sessions without negativity and imbalance, and which are shorter, more focused and constructive.

The over-use of commands can also become an inhibiting factor to a dog, and by withdrawing commands, adopting a silent approach and expecting less precision, your dog will come to enjoy its work far more. Aled Owen, the two times world champion, advocates ending a training session by allowing the dog to bring the sheep to the handler without command, to enable it to unwind before a session ends. He simply walks with his back to the sheep and dog, which inspires confidence in the dog that it is trusted to do the job without help or interference. Remember that feeling of exhilaration when you were first let loose with your father's prized tractor on your own? Where dogs are sensitive or anxious about aspects of work, giving frequent commands can serve to heighten their anxiety or sensitivity by putting them under greater pressure, especially if they are tired after a long session. Ideally, where young dogs are concerned, only once they have learned to cope with your methods of training and style of handling, including pressure movements, should you start to rely on commands.

Aled also, as a part of his everyday training, allows his dogs to get a natural feel for the sheep by not commanding them at the end of an outrun, leaving them instead to make the decision as to where to stop on the outrun, and how much pressure to use on the lift and fetch. By allowing this natural expression to take place a dog will learn more quickly than when you constantly shout or chastise it. The information will also be retained or consolidated for longer, as the dog will have acquired it naturally and on their own. (Information courtesy Aled Owen.)

My own dog Skerry was the type that had sensitive traits, but rarely was this prevalent where sheep work was concerned. As a two-year-old, Skerry came close to winning many

ABOVE: The stand-off.   *BELOW:* 'You're doing well' – just stick with it.

ABOVE: I said 'stick with *it', not stick* to *it!* *BELOW: 'Either way it worked.'*

trials, but failed either because she was not a confident shedding dog or did not have enough push at the pen. Yet by the time she was six years old she was patient enough to work flighty Welsh Mountain ewes or strong enough to handle mature and stubborn Scottish Blackface or Swaledale ewes with relative ease. Just as our scent is important to how our dogs perform, their scent or energy, and how they project it, is important to sheep. Skerry had the necessary armoury, and it was my job to help her realize this. I have noticed the same situation occur repeatedly with young gundogs that are blessed with the most wonderful scenting capabilities, who, whilst young, struggle to find objects because they are not confident or are lacking in trust in their own abilities.

Ultimately, a weak dog or one lacking in confidence, but which grows to find hidden strengths, might do a lot of winning at sheepdog trials ahead of a stronger dog that might be less precise or more forthright in its movements and easily upset sheep. Of course, what you must bear in mind is whether the former type of dog will do the same job for you on the farm.

THE UNKNOWN AND UNPREDICTABLE ASPECT OF DOGS

There is an awful lot that you will never read about in books, either because it defies belief or is difficult to make sense of. My twelve-year-old bitch Fly has so much respect for sheep to the point that she often ends up nose to nose with them, provided they are no threat to her. She has the patience of a saint. I recall running a flock of Manx Laughton into the shed once, and she ran in behind them, ready to put them through to a smaller drafting pen, before putting them through the race. A rather old ewe decided, despite Fly's gentle manner, that she didn't like Fly invading her personal space, and over the next hour she must have walked up to

Fly on four occasions and head butted her. Fly took the punishment but never retreated, other than to take evasive action; however, she didn't, at any point, show any aggression towards the old ewe. When I had finished with the sheep, I opened the gate into the yard and as the sheep started to walk out calmly, Fly ran to the old ewe, who was bringing up the rear and, totally unprovoked, nipped her just once on the hind leg, as if to say 'Don't you dare think you got one over on me!'

Fly's progeny have also demonstrated some surprising characteristics. I once found Spot lying in the garden motionless, but looking somewhat ill at ease. As I walked closer he didn't move. Finally as I reached him, I noticed, lying by his side, a baby thrush that had fallen out of the nest. As I picked it up, Spot sat up, sniffed it and gave it a gentle lick. Those people who know Spot on the trialling circuit know what a strong and powerful dog he is, and more than a handful, at times. Yet with those animals that are smaller or younger than him, he has shown the same sensitivity as with the baby thrush.

Of all the dogs I have owned, my cat Floss has a distinct liking for Spot and each morning she walks into the kitchen to greet him; yet the other dogs in the pack offer him far more respect, perhaps too much. Furthermore, each evening Spot also volunteers his services to put the rabbits away into what was the children's playhouse. Even when they object and are defiant in running into the playhouse, Spot demonstrates an uncanny patience, pacing in slow motion methodically until they are safely penned.

In the summer of 2004 I went into one of the fields on the Caudle estate, where Bryn and Marcus' sheep grazed. On walking into the field I could see a ewe lying perfectly still, in the middle of a ten-acre field. As I walked up to investigate, the ewe had also caught Fly's eye. Arriving at the same time, I noticed that she was still breathing and reached for my mobile phone

The gentle giant – Spot doing his evening job.

to ring Bryn. Whilst I was talking to him I noticed that Fly was taking a prolonged interest in the ewe, probably deciding whether a meal was to be had.

Fly is undoubtedly the greediest dog I have ever known and food is the greatest motivator in her life. However, she has morals and as such, she never considers anything as fair game or food unless she finds it to be dead, and some other bird or animal had started to eat it and drawn blood first. For Fly, our daily walk provides opportunities to go scavenging and little else, her head often buried in a rabbit hole or badger set.

By the time I'd finished talking to Bryn, Fly had, surprisingly, taken it upon herself to lie between the ewe's legs. A couple of minutes later the ewe died, whereupon Fly simply got up and went about her business as if nothing out of the ordinary had happened.

One of many contentious issues in Spot's training was when he was nine months old. He would go looking around the farm for sheep, defying any calls to come back – despite calling him repeatedly, he would fail to return to me and I would have to go and look for him. Having done this on several occasions I discovered that there was a theme developing. Each time I went looking for him, I usually discovered the cause of his behaviour: he was trying to tell me that a ewe or a lamb was in trouble and needed my attention. On one occasion I found him on a neighbouring farm lying next to a ewe that had got her head stuck through some fencing. Despite the harshness of my commands and insistence that he return to me, Spot had the resolve to stick to his guns and defy me, in the knowledge that he was right.

There are hidden aspects to every dog, some more so than others. Don't always assume that they are trying to wind you up or disobey you; learn to trust in your dog and your breeding. Even during daily work on the farm, you might find that your dog prefers to do things his or her way. Allow them this freedom to express themselves and see if they are trying to tell you something. These days, dogs are used in a variety of settings to help the blind, as sniffer dogs, to predict epileptic seizures, as home help and so on. By not assuming the worst and allowing time for your dogs to mature, develop and come to terms with the skills that are inbred, you will, hopefully, come to discover the genius within your dog.

The young of any species are curious, hungry for knowledge, and impetuous. They are bold and know no fear. By the time the pups are seven weeks old they are willing students when attention is given in the form of training, as long as it is pleasurable and rewarding. This is also an exciting time for the handler, as they gradually uncover the potential of their future champions.

Tess keen to work at fourteen weeks – what a relief!

CHAPTER 8

GENERAL OBEDIENCE

THE VALUE OF EARLY TRAINING

Training stimulates growth and forms a bond between us because it involves communication and interaction. A synergy emerges allowing both our dogs and ourselves to grow and learn in ways that are unique and might otherwise be impossible (Owens 2007).

When you undertake any form of training you must always keep in mind the elements of dominance, passive dominance and passive resistance discussed in earlier chapters. The early stages of training are the most crucial of any stage, and mistakes made here will affect performance at all subsequent stages. To mini-mize mistakes, all early obedience training should always take place with the dog on a lead.

It is crucial that you bring up your puppy or dog with a clear idea of what it can and can't do – of the rules. You will have to be firm with him: instil discipline, and this, combined with a little tender loving care, will lead to a very satisfying and fruitful partnership. Obedience shouldn't just mean 'do as I say': rather, it involves work-ing together and rewarding all that is positive, and ignoring all that is negative. Punishment does not enter this equation, and there is no place for it.

Using Treats

Dogs are highly motivated by food, therefore it should come as no surprise that they are happy to work for food. There are, however, some simple rules that must be followed when using food to train dogs:

- Never hide treats behind your back, as this will cause your dog to move and look for the treats.
- Treats belong to you, and by holding them in front of you, you are making a statement of dominance.
- Treats do not just represent food: rather, they represent anything that provokes a chase response in your dog. Treats can represent sheep, cattle, cars, motorbikes, cats and so on.
- By tossing a treat and catching it repeatedly you will encourage your dog to watch you and focus his attention on you for longer. This enables him to concentrate on the task at hand much better and for longer.
- If a treat is either thrown or accidently dropped, your dog must never be allowed to chase it or to pick up the treat from the floor. The treat must at all times be picked up by the handler and taken to the dog.
- In the early stages of training, treats can be given quite frequently; however, as training progresses, usually after three or four days,

they should be given randomly. Also you do not always have to give up the treat entirely; instead you can give your dog access to it by simply allowing it to taste the treat. This might seem preposterous to some, but how often do you allow your dog to kill a ewe and eat it afterwards? Never!

THE CHASE INSTINCT

The strongest instinct a dog has is the chase instinct, which stems from the need to hunt. This is responsible for any chasing behaviour, for example, when your dog chases livestock, traffic, or a cat or a tennis ball. This instinct is also responsible for other problem behaviours such as barking or sniffing the ground whilst walking on a lead. Even when you are trying to engage with your dog in a training exercise, if they fail to give you their attention, choosing instead to look at the sheep or other dogs, this is caused by the chase instinct. I also believe there is a link between a strong chase instinct and dogs that bark excessively.

The idea of controlling the chase instinct so early in a puppy's life is so that the chase can be controlled, and trust built up with the dog. You're not trying to stop the puppy from accessing the reward; rather there are certain conditions that he must satisfy first before you allow him access to the reward. This is exactly the same as teaching your dog not to chase sheep, wildly and uncontrollably, but to bring them in a calm manner that involves slow pacing rather than chasing. The best way in which to teach a puppy not to chase is to apply the 'no pull rule'.

The 'No Pull' Rule

This forms the basis of all your training. Whenever your puppy pulls towards anything (sheep, farm gates, dogs) it is your duty to ensure that he does not succeed. By allowing a puppy to pull, you are not only teaching it that pulling

works, but also that you are easily led or swayed.

If your puppy pulls as he gets older, this will be as a result of having been allowed to pull when he was young, and he has therefore learnt to have little regard for you. If you don't want your puppy to pull, then put a stop to it as soon as it occurs, and every time it occurs.

THE 'LISTEN' COMMAND

Obedience is strongly associated with attention, and therefore it makes sense to focus on getting the dog's attention before any other aspect of training progresses.

Teaching the 'Listen' Command

- With your dog on the lead, hold the very end of the lead and show your dog a treat. This can be a piece of dry food that your dog is fed on. You should be standing square on to the dog.
- Repeatedly throw the treat into the air and catch it: this will draw your dog's attention to you. Always hold the treat in front of you, and do not be tempted to hide it behind your back; this will merely make your dog curious and cause him to move and look for it. When your dog gives you his attention by looking at you and making eye contact, give the command 'Listen', and reward this behaviour by giving a treat on the command 'Take it'.
- Repeat the exercise until your dog looks at you on the command 'Listen'; within a few minutes he will learn that giving you his attention on the command 'Listen' leads to a reward. Men should be careful to deliver the command in a soft and gentle tone of voice – there is no need to shout!
- Treats should generally be given on the command 'Take it' or even 'Take hold', which in later training can be used to

invoke a controlled grip. This has the added benefit of teaching the dog that every other command other than 'Take it' implies that the dog should stay in the position he is in and not move forwards.

Attention is the key to success.

THE 'BALANCING' EXERCISE

The basis to this exercise is the very same as when teaching a young dog to balance sheep to the handler. Once your dog becomes familiar with it, he will recognize the same movements when working with sheep, and hopefully respond in a favourable manner.

The balancing exercise is designed not only to teach your dog to walk on the lead properly, but also to stop when you stop, to give you his undivided attention, and also to stay in a given position. It is a multifaceted exercise, and the benefits can only be gained by repeating it over a number of weeks.

Teaching the Balancing Exercise

- In the early stages don't worry too much about using commands, but practise getting your dog to 'listen'. Bait your dog with a treat, holding it centrally and not to the side. When he looks at you, give him a treat and give the command 'Listen'.
- Then using his name, pull him gently by the lead towards you until he starts to move, and take a step or two backwards.
- Bringing the treat down to the dog's mouth, turn clockwise, still walking backwards, and take up the position your dog was in at the beginning of the exercise.
- Then repeat the exercise, but making sure that when you turn you do so in an anti-clockwise manner. Give a treat when your dog comes to a standstill and looks at you, on the command 'Listen'.

If you should go wrong and turn anti-clockwise at the beginning, then ensure that the second turn is in a clockwise direction. If you have done the exercise correctly you will have done a figure-of-eight with your dog; if you have done it incorrectly, then you will end up doing a circle.

THE 'STAND' COMMAND

For everyday work and for trials I prefer a dog that works on its feet rather than lies down. However, some dogs that are strong or simply exuberant when they are young, tend to put too much pressure on sheep whilst on their feet, and need to be taught to lie down.

It is always best to keep your options open and train dogs both to lie down and to stand. Some dogs tend to stand quite naturally, and this tendency is evident even as young as twelve weeks; usually they are naturally wide running and flanking dogs that don't pressurize sheep. Most dogs, however, when they are away from sheep and the thrill of the chase, will stand quite well, without gaining ground or taking advantage.

When training young dogs at home I often use the 'Stand' command. I am also always careful to correct any movement forwards, as in trials competition a single movement forwards can lead to a missed obstacle, pen or shed and so the consequences are significantly higher. Often, however, if a young dog is given a 'Stand' command and it moves forwards, if it is corrected the extra pressure placed on it will have the effect of making it lie down. Both dogs and handlers need time to read and deliver pressure correctly, and only through practice can the correct pressure be applied without adverse effects (*see* Chapter 9).

Regarding pen work, it is also crucial that dogs are taught to make only small movements towards the sheep, and also, if they happen to lie down, to get up slowly so as not to upset

Holding a treat to the mouth will keep a dog standing.

them. Dogs with even a small degree of eye will do this naturally.

As dogs gain in confidence and experience, it is not uncommon that they will choose to stay on their feet, and as long as their movement is controlled, I prefer this sort of continuity over stopping and starting. In the course of a sheepdog trial or working on the farm, the objective is to get the job done in the quickest and most efficient manner, but a dog that is constantly up and down will not only unsettle the sheep each time it jumps back up, it will also tire more quickly.

Teaching the 'Stand' Command

- Stand with the dog either by your side or in front of you. Then, using the 'Listen' command to get his attention, toss the treat at arm's length, and catch it again to keep the dog's focus on you. Ensure that he does not, or cannot move forwards to chase the treat. If he stands, give the command 'Stand' and continue to toss/catch the treat.

- If you find that your dog does not like to stand, or sits down, to prevent this happening take a treat to his mouth just when you think he is about to sit or lie down, slightly drawing it forwards.

- Once the dog stands comfortably and does not make any attempt to sit down, you are now ready to progress to the next stage. Stand the dog and hold a treat at arm's length. Then, ensuring that the dog cannot or does not move forwards, give the command 'Stand' and throw the treat about half a metre away, or far enough for you to reach with ease.

- Then after a few seconds, pick up the treat and hold it at arm's length and repeat the 'Stand' command frequently. If the dog continues to stand, then move the treat closer, again repeating the 'Stand' command.

- Finally take the treat to the dog's mouth, and if he does not attempt to eat the treat, or averts his eyes or moves his head to one side, reward this by giving the treat on the 'Take it' command. If your dog does try and mouth the treat, repeat the 'Stand' command as soon as he moves towards the treat.

Remember that the 'Stand' command also means 'Stay', so the treat should be away from the dog whenever this command is used. This ensures that whenever you give either the 'Stand' or 'Lie down' commands, you are also reinforcing the fact that your dog should not move until he is given a release command such as 'That's enough'. Some people may choose to use 'That'll do' to signify the end of an exercise; however, I prefer this to mean 'Come to me', and 'That's enough' to signify 'Stop what you're doing'.

This exercise should only take a minute or so to complete, and should be repeated two to

Tip

Once your dog stops chasing the treat or there is no tension on the lead, remember to keep the lead loose and put the pressure on your dog. Only tighten the lead either to stop the dog from chasing the treat, or when you think it might chase the treat.

three times. Once your dog stops chasing the treat, you are ready to throw it further and gradually build the distance from your dog, as well as the time away from your dog. If at any time you think your dog is about to move, you must return to him instantly and start again. Remember to repeat the 'Stand' command until you finally return to your dog and reward him for staying. As training progresses you can give the treats randomly.

THE 'DOWN' COMMAND

There are some instances when I would remain cautious about teaching a dog to lie down. Some dogs, known as 'clappers', instinctively lie down when they are uncertain, and this type of dog can be difficult to work with any fluency: they don't need an excuse to lie down, so it is preferable that they are kept on their feet and moving. A dog that lies down without a

command, and at the wrong time, can cost just as many points at a trial as a dog that fails to lie down at all and is out of control.

Teaching the 'Down' Command

▦ Hold a treat in front of you and move it to your dog's nose, then slowly move it above his head and this will encourage him to sit. Then take the treat slowly past the dog's nose, in a straight line to the floor, by his feet. Your dog should follow the treat to the floor and lie down. You may give a treat as it lies down, saying 'Take it' or 'Take hold'. Don't worry about using commands such as 'Sit' or 'Down' just yet.

▦ Alternatively you can do the above exercise straight from the standing position by moving the treat in exactly the same way.

▦ Only once your dog becomes fluent and lies down quickly should you start to use the 'Lie down' command. Remember, when your dog sits it is not necessary to use the 'Sit' command unless you want to teach the sit as a separate exercise.

It might be necessary for you to crouch down next to your dog, prior to moving the treat away. However, you should try and achieve a standing position as soon as your dog is comfortable in the down position, and not likely to move

Take the treat from the mouth to the feet and the dog will lie down.

Tip

Avoid pushing or forcing the dog down with your hands as this will cause him to mistrust you and become hand shy. Rather than being impatient, concentrate on the stand exercise until your dog becomes more confident.

instantly. By initially holding on to the treat, you can quickly return it to your dog's mouth when you think it might get up.

Remember, as with the stand exercise, only give a 'Lie down' command once your dog lies down and when the treat is away from him.

Teaching the 'Down and Stay'

Once your dog is lying down, in order to progress further, carry out the following exercise:

- Lie your dog down as above and crouch down next to him. If he looks settled, then start by giving the 'Lie down' command. Then while repeating it, throw a treat about a foot away. Continue repeating the command throughout.
- After five seconds, pick up and take the treat to the dog, first half way, then to his mouth. Only give the treat if he does not attempt to eat it, when he averts his eyes or moves his head to one side, on the 'Take it' command.
- As the dog becomes more confident, you can throw the treat a little further. If you feel at any time that your dog might get up or move, then quickly pick up the treat or have a second treat ready, to take to the dog in order to stop the movement. Gradually your dog will come to understand the 'Stand' and 'Down' commands.

Whether you are training a dog to lie down or to

stand, keep the task simple and build up the time gradually, starting initially with as little as five seconds, and progressing to longer times. In addition to increasing the times, you should also increase the distance you throw the treat, anything up to three to six metres. As well as moving away from your dog you should also practise circling your dog, as this manoeuvre will be used in later training when working in a training pen.

Whether you are training the 'Stand' command or the 'Down', it is not necessary to use the 'Stay' command. Remember when you give either command, 'Stay' is implied automatically. Your dog should only move when he is given a release command such as 'That's enough' or 'That'll do'.

At any time during the 'Stand' or 'Down' exercise, if you think the dog might be about to move, take the treat back to their mouth and say 'Take it' or 'Take hold', as appropriate.

Once you have trained your dog to lie down and can move a considerable distance away from him, as described above, you are now ready to progress to the next step: to get your dog to lie down, without taking a treat to the

Throw the treat and return with it, and reward the dog for standing still.

Guiding Principle

Please note and remember that dog training is such an intricate art that by certain inappropriate actions you could be training both desirable and undesirable behaviours simultaneously.

---

floor, from an upright position, and without using a command first. This will normally be about four or five weeks from when training commenced.

Teaching the 'Down' without Command

- Stand with the dog in front of you. Then using the 'Listen' command, to get his attention toss the treat at arm's length, and catch it again to keep the dog's focus on you. Use no other commands at all. Ensure that the dog does not or cannot move forwards to chase the treat. Ensure that his attention remains on you only, correcting any deviations, by taking a treat to his mouth.
- Each time you take the treat to the dog's mouth give the 'Listen' command and instantly pull the treat back, ensuring the dog does not get access to it, at all.
- Continue doing this and you will notice your dog's attention improving. Its head might even start to drop a little. Any movements you observe on your dog's face will reflect the thought processes he is going through, trying to work out what you want, and what he needs to do next.
- In approximately 60 per cent of cases, with a variety of dog breeds, dogs soon lie down without any command, when baited this way. This is achieved by a process of elimination, by not rewarding the dog for either a sit or a stand movement. In Border Collies

the success rate is higher, approximately 75 per cent.
- As soon as the dog lies down, instantly reward it with a treat, and give a 'Lie down' command simultaneously.
- As you repeat this exercise, your dog will lie down a lot more quickly. Eventually, even when you say 'Listen', this will invoke a 'down' response.
- Once your dog lies down with great regularity, tether him to a fence and repeat the exercise, this time giving the command from a distance, a metre away, then two, and three, until you are up to six metres away, or further if you wish.

Eventually, as your puppy learns the 'Lie down' command, it will take all commands willingly, particularly when you give the command in a group setting, with your other dogs present. Young dogs will watch how the older dogs are behaving, and mimic their behaviour. I have found that approximately 10 per cent of dogs will lie down almost instantly when presented with a treat as above, even without any form of 'stand' or 'down' training taking place before hand. The great majority of these are Border Collies.

HOW OFTEN SHOULD DOGS BE OBEDIENCE TRAINED?

Young pups will only be able to concentrate on any given task for a few minutes, therefore it is essential that all the training exercises described above last only five minutes or so in total. They should, however, be repeated three to four times daily. As with all forms of training, whether it be with puppies or adult dogs, the occasional break from training can also prove beneficial for both handler and dog. Although it is important to ensure consistency, it is just as important to ensure that boredom does not set in, as this will be counter-productive.

CHAPTER 9

THE 'PRESSURE ON, PRESSURE OFF' TECHNIQUE

MONTY ROBERTS, 'THE MAN WHO LISTENS TO HORSES'

Many years ago in the early 1990s I happened to watch a television programme featuring a new phenomenon in the world of horse training. Although I have never had any interest in horses I was nevertheless intrigued by the way in which he was working with wild horses. The man was Monty Roberts, otherwise known as 'the man who listens to horses'. When Monty was young, he observed, whilst tracking wild mustangs, a non-verbal communication between the horses, which he later named 'Equus'.

Using this, Monty developed a means of communicating with horses through body language. He called this 'Join-Up', which was founded on 'consistent principles, communication and trust'. Most important of all, Monty asserted that 'violence is never the answer'. (Courtesy Monty Roberts, *The Man Who Listens to Horses*, see References.)

I marvelled at how Monty, within a short space of time, was able to gain the trust of a wild and untrained mustang through the application and withdrawal of pressure. Quite simply by walking towards the horse and giving full eye contact, and vice versa, Monty was able to send

Monty Roberts performing join-up.

Guiding Principle

'Be the change you want to see in the world.'   Mahatma Gandhi

Meeting Monty at Myerscough College, Preston.

the horse galloping around the corral, bucking and kicking its hind legs, as it ran from him. Yet no sooner had he stopped, it too stopped. As he turned his back on the horse, thereby totally withdrawing the pressure, and started to move in the opposite direction, the horse instinctively was drawn to Monty and started to follow him. Each time Monty came to a halt, so did the horse, until after several minutes the horse finally plucked up enough courage to keep moving towards Monty, and made physical contact with him. Walking up to a very still and relaxed Monty, the horse sniffed him on the back of his head, to glean some information about him.

The crowd was awestruck, as was I, and my mind was now filled with questions about how I could apply similar principles to training dogs. If horses had their own way of communicating with each other, then so too would dogs. Observation of dogs, therefore, became the most critical tool in discovering how they communicated with one another. Although I haven't always practised the following sentiment, especially in my youth, experience has taught me that we

should try and understand not only the Border Collie, but each other. Rather than trying to inflict our own values and ways on to others, we should instead focus on understanding and changing ourselves.

For your collie to listen to you in a field full of running sheep, it must first of all become accustomed not only to hearing the same commands whilst away from sheep, but also to reading and becoming accustomed to your body language and associated smell, pheromone or energy.

As stated earlier, all forms of change will always be met with some resistance, and if that process is deemed to be a fair one, then the resistance will take a less intense form and eventually change will be embraced.

APPLYING THE PRESSURE ON, PRESSURE OFF TECHNIQUE

Pressure is a necessary tool in training dogs, and contrary to common belief, it can also be applied to dogs that are of a sensitive nature as well as to hard dogs. At the end of the day, if a dog's behaviour or intention is to kill sheep or, inadvertently, it causes injury or stress to sheep,

Guiding Principle

'Power is of two kinds. One is obtained by the fear of punishment, and the other by acts of love. Power based on love is a thousand times more effective and permanent then the one derived from fear of punishment.'   Mahatma Gandhi

The feeling is mutual.

then you have no choice but to take necessary steps to ensure that the sheep do not come to any harm. However, where you do have a choice is how you deal with such dogs, and as with Monty Roberts, I believe that there is no room for violence.

The solution in many instances lies in the application of the 'pressure on, pressure off' technique, and the types of pressure that can be applied to a dog can take the following forms:

- Fixed and full-on eye contact.
- Silence.
- Stern use of the voice, a gruff voice or a deep growl.
- Use of tension on the lead or long line.
- Moving towards a dog forcefully, or with purpose, or running.
- Close proximity combined with an assertive, dominant stance/posture.
- The use of noise aversion, such as a loud voice or the rustling of a bag.
- Blocking the dog's forward movement.

In all cases, whenever pressure of any kind is applied, the handler must observe the following rules:

- Pressure must be applied within the first two seconds of undesired behaviour occurring. Don't hold a grudge.

- As soon as the desired behaviour is achieved – the dog stops or looks away – you must cease to apply further pressure. If you have moved towards your dog to exert pressure, you must stop instantly the dog reacts or stops; however, you need not move back to your starting point and totally withdraw. When pressure is maintained and not retracted the dog will often move, thereby releasing the pressure themselves.
- You do not always need to insist on your dog lying down during an exercise, as sometimes a glance away or a deflected movement away from the sheep is better, as it enables you to provide continuity. Continuity ensures that you will have to put less pressure on your dog. It also leads to your dog gaining in confidence and experiencing an adrenalin rush.
- Pressure of any kind must not be abused.

If you continue to move towards your dog once they have corrected their behaviour, they will become confused and in some cases will stop working or will run away from you. Your dog will also perceive your behaviour as bullying and threatening, and will cease to work willingly. If you happen to be carrying a crook, stick or any other object, you will risk your dog associating your actions with those objects, and it is highly likely that at some time in the future, probably during a sheepdog trial, your dog will choose to repay you.

Exercise One

- Place on the floor any object that your dog is highly motivated by, such as a food bowl, bone, or even some sheep wool.
- Walk your dog, on a lead, towards the article and when you are a metre or so away, drop the lead. Your dog will make a move for the article and try and obtain it by bulldozing, nose down first, and harassing you.

The level of intensity they show at this stage is a measure of the respect they hold for you, or in this case, lack of respect.

- Protect the article by blocking any movement towards it with your feet. Maintain an upright posture and face the dog, remaining calm and silent. You might end up doing an Irish jig, but very soon your dog will stop and reassess the situation. It will either give up, or it might decide to have one more go, or even several. Gradually, however, it will give up. Verbal commands are not necessary and may convey a different meaning to that which was intended.

- Once your dog moves away from the article you should also take a step away (learning to forgive). Watch the dog's face closely, and counter any movement by blocking the dog and stepping in towards the article. This will cause your dog to step back. You can either continue to extend the distance away from the article by continuing to walk towards the dog, or you can withdraw the pressure totally.

- Your actions, whether they maintain or withdraw pressure, along with the degree of pressure, should be proportionate to the level of intensity your dog shows. Sometimes you might need to walk in or step in firmly, and at other times if greater distance is involved you might need to run. Easygoing pups will not need a lot of pressure or practice before they concede.

- If you are using food, at the point when your dog stops hassling you and either chooses to stand still or lies down, pick up the food and give him some of it. If your dog stands, continuing to hold the food bowl in your hand may also cause him eventually to lie down. If you are using a toy or piece of wool, pick it up and allow controlled access to it – allow the dog to take the toy gently without snatching, or to sniff the wool calmly. By holding

Eyes averted as a mark of respect for the handler.

an object close to your dog's face and only allowing access you are establishing your leadership: when he turns his head away or avert his eyes, he is signifying acceptance and acknowledgement of your leadership.

- Only introduce commands when the desired behaviour is achieved and not before. Commands are instructions, so do not plead or beg.

- Practise this exercise at least twice daily until your dog gives in totally.

If your dog starts to pull severely towards the article, then return to the starting point, or go even further back and start again, holding the end of the lead and trying to maintain a loose lead at all times. Your dog will soon work out that pulling merely delays the opportunity to get to the article. This is a good way of teaching your dog to walk on the lead without pulling.

You must, however, remain sensitive to your dog's emotions and mental state. Remember you want your dog to be on your side, and trust must always be maintained.

Exercise Two

This exercise involves placing your dog outside a room it likes to be in, or the other side of a gateway into a field or training pen with sheep in, which it desperately wants to get into. You need not partly close the gate/door or even hold on to it, although with some highly intense dogs this may be necessary.

- Block with your legs, as above, any attempts by the dog to barge past you.
- Maintain a calm, upright posture.
- Your dog will make repeated attempts to come through, but will soon realize your objective. Normally when it concedes it will move backwards, lie down, sit or stand still. It will also make eye contact.
- Only once the dog concedes should you invite them in, quietly, and being sure to block any sharp/quick movements.
- Every movement inwards from your dog must be met with counter pressure towards them.

This exercise is exactly what you should do when allowing your dog to enter a training pen with sheep. Once the dog enters the pen you should ask it to lie down for a few seconds until it is calm before proceeding.

Regarding any form of pressure, if you do not withdraw it, you cannot apply it again. By not withdrawing pressure you will cause the situation to become more intense, which is not appropriate. Remember, you don't have to win every battle, but you do have to fight every battle. If you choose to ignore any aspect of behaviour you are giving licence for your dog to do as it wishes. Any silence or objection that you fail to voice or convey will be perceived as your granting permission to behave badly.

Before introducing your dog to sheep it is a good idea to establish good stops in the form of your dog lying down, and good recalls. At approximately six months of age, or a month before introducing sheep work, you should focus your training on achieving a good stop. During regular daily walks each day periodically ask all the dogs to lie down (assuming you have

Tess learns to lie down by watching the older dogs.

more than one). More often than not the pups will watch the others and learn from them. If, however, they are hesitant or refuse, take a few steps towards them and repeat the 'Lie down' command once more. Remember that by six months of age, your dogs should be fully versed with the 'Lie down' and 'Stand' commands. You can give praise verbally, or just give a release command. You can use the same method to deal with any refusal when your dog is recalled or if a dog is barking unnecessarily. As soon as the dog realizes that that refusal is not an option and that you will reinforce any commands you give, they will be less likely to ignore you.

Once you have introduced the above training you can apply the same methods when you start to train your dog for the first time on sheep. The times when pressure can or needs to be applied are as follows:

Controlling access into a field before gathering sheep.

■ When you walk to the field where the sheep are – make the dog walk behind you and do not allow him to race ahead. If necessary ask him to lie down, and counter any excessive changes of speed.
■ When you leave your dog to send him on to a short gather.
■ When he refuses to lie down.
■ When he comes in tight on the flanks.
■ When he fails to come away from the sheep and recall.

You won't always need to rely on physical pressure, and sometimes delivering a strong command will achieve the desired result.

If you have let your dog get away with elements of poor behaviour either because you did not spot the signs or because you were not prepared to apply pressure on them, your dog will grow to disregard you as a weaker member of the partnership and consequently will disregard your part when working sheep. He will happily flank into your 'zone', or will even cut in and flank in front of you. His flanks, either on one side or both, will be inadequate, and he will refuse to lie down or come back when called.

Learn to read your dog's body language: erect ears, head, tail, nose up are all heightened senses, which must be acted on when observed. These signs signify a thought entering your dog's head, which must be acted on instantly in order to prevent bad behaviour from occurring. If you are too late and a particular behaviour does occur, you will have two seconds to respond otherwise your dog will ignore you.

If the early obedience training and pressure techniques applied are successful, they will pave a smooth path for the pup to start working with sheep. The pup will recognize your commands and your posture, and will be less likely to experience stress, and more likely to enjoy the beginnings of a new relationship with sheep.

Portrait of a Successful Handler – Tim Longton

Tim Longton describes in his own words what it takes to become a successful handler, and the types of dog that make successful sheepdogs.

Success comes from many different strands. For me, being born to such a successful trialling and sheep farming family that has been competing at international level for four generations has been a significant factor. The Longton name is well known and respected throughout the world. My grandfather was the first Tim, followed by his sons Will, Tot, Tim, Jim, Bob and Jack, who all competed at some level.

The principles of training are quite simple, and whilst you can explain the theory, the art of getting the most from the dog only comes with experience and knowing how sheep will react to different types of dog.

Working with dogs to a high standard needs a lot of consistency, time and training – you can't say don't do something one day and then allow it the next – and knowing which dogs to apply pressure to when training and which dogs to encourage. The timing of pressure and encouragement are important, and because I have been around sheep and dogs all my life, these things have become almost as instinctive as the dog working the sheep.

Work with the dogs on extensive hills and large fields gives an advantage at national and international-style trials, but can be a disadvantage at small trials where the pressure the dog puts on to the sheep causes problems. The successful dog has to be a blend of natural ability and trainability. I have had success with

Tim Longton – the pedigree of the handler can be just as important as that of the dog!

both dogs and bitches. Both have their pluses and minuses.

I like a dog/bitch that has a natural feel for its sheep, and which can control sheep with a quiet authority, being fearless but not aggressive. Trials work requires an extremely good temperament, as one day you can be in a small field with a few other handlers, and another day you can be stood in front of a grandstand full of people with a public address system working and other distractions.

(Information courtesy of Timothy Longton.)

CHAPTER 10

EARLY TRAINING WITH SHEEP

STARTING WITH SHEEP

Teaching your Pup to Look for Sheep

Prior to starting any work with sheep, it is essential that your dog has learnt to lie down, to stand and to come when called, at a reasonable distance – say, six to twelve metres. You should also introduce some basic whistle commands to stop and recall your dog. Of course the 'Stand' command may work well whilst you are away from livestock, but when you start training on sheep, it will probably not be as precise. You should therefore use the 'Down' command initially, and when your dog is a little steadier and less boisterous, you can revert to using the 'Stand' command again.

Before you start any formal training, it is a good idea to introduce your young puppy to sheep. Early contact with sheep enables the handler to determine the type of pup they have, as well as giving the pup a chance to learn about sheep, both informally and without any pressure. This is an important part of the early socializing process, on which I place the greatest emphasis.

Introducing the 'Look' Command

Each time you take a young pup to sheep, watch him closely until he looks directly at them or shows any interest, and then introduce the 'Look' command. Ensure that you are standing square on and facing the sheep. Some dogs will look at you as soon as you speak, so only use the 'Look' command when the dog looks directly at the sheep.

He will come to associate the command and position with the direction of the sheep. Later on, when you start his sheep training, he will already be familiar with the 'Look' command. Your physical position will serve as a non-verbal signal as to where to look for the sheep, and this will prove extremely useful, not just in everyday farm work, especially when gathering over large areas or over moorland, but also at sheepdog trials. As training progresses, by saying 'Look' your dog will be aware that there are sheep in the field and that he is about to work. Furthermore, the 'Look' command will also prepare your dog for later, more advanced training when you teach a blind outrun (when the sheep are out of sight).

You can also put the 'Look' command to good use should your dog be faced with a difficult ewe, one that is facing up to him, or if your dog takes his eyes off the sheep. The 'Look' command focuses the dog's eyes directly on to the challenging ewe, thereby putting more pressure on the ewe to yield and move on.

As with all training situations, it is far better to put a command or give a name to an action that your dog is in the process of performing; this

Mules and Hebrideans – experience of different breeds of sheep is crucial.

way you are not telling him to do something, rather, you are giving his actions a name.

How Many Sheep to Use

Initially it is best to start with a dozen or so sheep depending on the breed and how dogged they are. Young dogs need to be able to keep up with sheep, should they take off, and also they need to be able to move them easily, and with confidence. Heavy lowland breeds of sheep tend to stand in the middle of the field and offer little or no challenge to the dog; I prefer free-moving sheep that educate young dogs and provide an experience more similar to what they will find at sheepdog trials.

As training progresses, however, the more sheep you have the better, as this makes it easier to teach the dog to widen the flanks (the act of covering sheep) – and the more spread out the sheep are, the further the dog will have to open out and flank. Furthermore, once your dog learns to gather larger flocks of sheep you will be able to use him for practical work on the farm, which will broaden his experience.

Dealing with a Gripper

For any young dog, his early training experiences will set the precedent for later success or failure. This will also be dictated by his own character, and the type of dog you prefer: thus you might be quite happy with a young dog that runs riot, causing sheep to run in every direction and leaving bits of wool all over the field, or this type of dog might be a nightmare to you. Like many triallists, I prefer this type of dog as I strongly believe that it is much easier to slow a dog down than it is to inject pace and urgency into his work. Also this type of dog does eventually slow down – as unfortunately does an easygoing dog, too, sometimes running wider and losing touch with their sheep, or not having enough presence to command respect.

In 1989, I purchased a daughter by Sydney Price's Davy, called Lara. Although she ran out well on both sides, she was incredibly hard on lifting sheep, and inevitably came in and gripped a ewe. She sometimes hung on for dear life, with her hind legs and small frame occasionally lifting off the ground as she struggled to keep pace.

Having read various books on the matter, the only advice I could find was not to be too hard on the dog too early, thereby putting it off sheep altogether. Having repeatedly watched videos of Lara's assault on sheep, I struggled to find a solution – until one day the problem was resolved almost by chance. She had chased the sheep into a corner of the field, and since we were all out of breath and panting heavily,

myself the most, I decided to let Lara hold the sheep in the corner for a moment while I sat down to catch my breath. Lara took up a position about three metres or so from the sheep and held them there, not daring to enter their personal space. Then suddenly, something remarkable happened: as I sat down and relaxed, making myself comfortable, Lara did just the same, first sitting, but soon following with a down position. As she relaxed, the expression on the sheep became less intense and they gradually began to gain trust and even looked away from her.

Ten minutes later the occasional ewe started to graze, and Lara's eyes, in turn, became less fixated on the sheep and began to look less intent and aggressive. I then asked her to move closer to the sheep; initially she was happy to get up on her feet, but she didn't move forwards. Gradually, however, she did creep forwards, though painfully slowly; so when she

Lara – a daughter of Sidney Price's Davy.

'I heard one of the dogs say something about averting the eyes.'

was but a metre or so from the sheep, I called her off, then asked her to walk towards them once more. This took the pressure off both her and the sheep, allowing each party to regroup and refocus. This time she was less hesitant, and the sheep were less startled. Then moving to one side, I called Lara to me, thereby releasing the pressure on the far side and allowing the sheep to make a calm retreat, rather than a hasty one.

As I saw a gap develop between the sheep and the fence, I asked Lara to run through and fetch the sheep back. The amazing thing was that she ran between the fence and sheep under control, so as not to spook or hassle them. Having run past them, she brought them back into the corner, a picture of infinite calm and serenity – just like the scene from the film *Babe*, when Pig lifted the sheep at the sheepdog trial, amidst the hush of the crowd.

I was amazed to see that we had spent nearly thirty minutes working through this episode, but most surprising was how calm and shallow my breathing was. I was just as focused and calm as the sheep and Lara, and this way of overcoming probably potentially the most fraught of all exercises inspired me to use this approach in other aspects of training. Over the next few days I repeated this way of training with Lara until the problem was completely resolved.

This exercise became a regular part of my training routine, particularly when breaking in young dogs, and time and again it has been successful. In some cases I have placed the sheep in a small pen with the dog immediately on the outside, and at other times I have taken the dog inside the pen.

This coming together of two different species is no different to strangers coming together in a waiting room or a lift. Initially there is an

ABOVE: *Young dogs need their 'hands holding' sometimes to face their fears.*

RIGHT: *Let go off the lead and allow the dog to run through once it looks away from the sheep.*

teaching the flanks. To teach the flank, proceed in the following way:

- Whilst the dog is lying or standing on the outside of the pen, repeat the stop command and move the sheep (inside the pen) away from the dog in the opposite direction. This will require a big flank. Once you have moved the sheep you can then step back and shush the dog to move. Most young dogs will, however, automatically move as the sheep move. As they flank, remain slightly behind the line between the dog and sheep (line A in the diagram below), and follow them round.
- When the dog gathers pace and is about to overtake the sheep and head them, stop yourself, then double back in the opposite direction so that you meet the dog coming towards you. Once the dog has gone past the last ewe he will come to a halt or slow down, particularly if he sees you coming towards him. The idea is that your dog learns to stop once all the sheep have been covered – that is, once he has moved past

all the sheep. By moving into a position where your dog can see you, also past the sheep, you are providing a visual signal for him to stop.

- The moment your dog comes to a halt, raise your arm above your head: this will give him another non-verbal signal to stop, which will be particularly useful when you use a bigger flock later on. Try to avoid asking your dog to lie down when he is in 'full flow': instead, wait for him to slow down or stop first, before giving a stop command.
- Once the dog comes to accept and understand your movements, you can then apply the reverse and practise the opposite flank.

The diagram shows the position you need to be in whilst your dog is flanking in an anti-clockwise direction. Once your dog starts to flank to its right, imagine a line A from the dog to the sheep, shown in the centre of the pen. Move in the same direction as the dog, but remain slightly behind the line A – thus from B to C, then C to D, D to E and so on. Move swiftly, remaining behind line A, and you will notice that whilst your dog is running in a circle, your movement is a square, as shown.

Keep the dog moving around the pen once or even twice, then when you are ready to ask him to stop – as he almost reaches E – double back from position C to B, ensuring the sheep are not directly between you and your dog (they should be to your right-hand side). As the dog sees you coming towards him, he will come to a halt automatically, and lie down or stand. If, on the other hand, you ask your dog to stop when either he or you are behind the sheep, he will be more focused on the sheep and will ignore your commands. You should remember this movement whether you are using a training pen or not, and whether your dog is working inside or outside the pen. By maintaining the square movement you will ensure that you do not get in

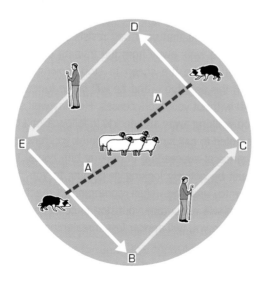

Follow your dog from B to C, C to D and so on, remaining behind line A. The line A moves as the dog moves.

line with your dog and the sheep (A) and inadvertently cause him either to stop or to change direction. If your dog does change direction, you may already have made this mistake.

Whilst using the square movement you must ensure that you walk towards the dog until you are within three metres or so from him, and your physical presence will ensure that your dog does not cut in towards the sheep.

The square movement method is also ideal for a dog that doesn't flank freely, is too slow or hesitant, and for a dog that 'eyes' sheep up. Your movement behind him will serve to put gentle pressure on him to keep moving, and provides him with the necessary momentum. If you see him slowing down, or even about to stop when you don't want him to, moving forcefully towards him and/or giving him a firm command to flank will keep him mobile and teach him to be fluent. A free-flanking dog is a godsend – provided he comes with good brakes!

Do not make the mistake of assuming that the square position is a fixed position: keep the concept in your mind but maintain some flexibility, and this will ensure you are in the right place all the time. This cannot be an exact science, simply because all the factors do not always hold constant. Remember to keep the sheep in the centre of the pen, where possible, and avoid getting too close to them. By allowing a metre or two gap between you and the sheep as you move round, you are leaving them with space to move into if your dog is too tight.

Tip

The golden rule is, that whatever distance you adopt away from the sheep, your dog will adopt either the same or a greater distance from the sheep also. Therefore the wider you move, the wider your dog will learn to run/flank.

As your dog's instincts to work become stronger and more intense, you will generally find that he will start to predict your movements, and to counteract your movements and change direction. He will also refuse to lie down. This is perfectly natural, and only by working through this intensity and staying calm will your dog come to realize that he cannot progress without your help. Rather than fighting with your dog by insisting he lies down, just stand still and wait for the sheep to stop moving. Once they stop, so will the dog. Avoid becoming animated, stay calm, and concentrate on keeping moving.

BRINGING THE DOG INSIDE THE PEN

Once you are confident that your dog understands what you are trying to achieve, and also when he has had an opportunity to release excess energy, you can consider bringing him inside the pen. Of course this will serve to intensify his reactions, which is why it is all the more important to remember the points mentioned previously regarding your preparations for starting work with sheep.

Once inside the pen, it is crucial that you learn to read not only your dog, but the sheep also. Remember, you are also part of the equation, and what you do and how you behave will either make or break the level of success you achieve. Therefore before you take the dog into the pen it might also be a good idea to mark out the movements on your own so that you are clear about what you need to achieve. When your dog is working inside the pen, there is less time for you to think and to make decisions. Often you cannot pre-plan what you will do next, as your actions are determined by what your dog and the sheep do next. You must remain calm, yet focused all the time, and above all you must move constantly to allow the sheep room inside the pen to feel safe. The only time you should be standing still is when you give your dog the command to flank, but thereafter you must remain mobile and be fluent.

Your positioning is the key to your dog getting continuity, and therefore becoming less frustrated. For a dog, continuity of work is far better than being praised. Furthermore, if your movements are positive and decisive, then you will also inspire confidence in the sheep, and before long you will find that they, too, will seek protection from you, by following you. Sheep work is a partnership between man and dog, and each has their own part to play; thus a dog that differentiates his role from that of his masters will be a calmer, well organized worker.

Your dog will also come to realize that it is his duty to look after one half of the training pen, and your duty is to look after your half. Later when you work outside the training pen the same will apply. This will enable your dog to rest, and it will also teach him that there are times when you can move the sheep on your own, without needing his help. If done correctly this exercise will prove invaluable later on while in the shedding ring or when you need to leave the dog a good distance away, whilst examining, say, a pregnant ewe.

Correcting Problems

Whilst working in and outside a pen, I use a home-made implement constructed from a carrier bag and a rolled-up newspaper (the handle), which enables me to make visual as well as audible contact with the dog, as the dog's attention will be focused on the sheep. The rolled-up newspaper is taped with parcel tape to keep it dry, and the carrier bag – thin and rustling from a supermarket – is taped at one end. Such a tool is not intended to threaten the dog in any way: rather, it is used to deflect his attention or interrupt his thought pattern away from the sheep, to break his concentration and remind him of my presence. The bag also enables me to remain vocally quiet during the early stages of training.

Whilst your dog is flanking, if he turns his head inwards, towards the sheep, give a flank or a stop command because looking in is the first step to coming in. Remember, deal with the thought, not the behaviour, and a dog that is starting to look in towards the sheep is at the first stage of a problem about to occur, because looking in will be followed by him coming in tighter on the flank. If a dog is too tight or about to grip, throw the bag in front of him to prevent a grip – but once again, try to remain silent at this early stage. Once the dog starts to flank correctly, refrain from carrying any object.

Prior to starting work inside the pen, bring your dog into the pen calmly, ensuring he walks in slowly and without lunging at the sheep, as above. Once in the pen, give a firm 'Lie down' command. This is crucial, because this will be the dog's first contact with the sheep inside the pen, and a 'statement of ownership' of the sheep is instantly conveyed by giving firm commands. By now you will know which side they prefer to run in, so choose to send them in this direction because your dog will then be more confident. Then try to break the dog's attention from the sheep by rustling the bag each time it looks at them with intent. Soon the dog will realize that you do not want it to look at the sheep. Ensuring that the sheep are in the middle of the pen, only give the shushing command to start the dog off once it looks away from the sheep. If the dog goes round the sheep, follow close behind, taking great care not to cross the imaginary line between the dog and the sheep. Also ensure that the sheep remain in the middle of the pen, by keeping a safe distance from them as you move round the pen. A dog that flanks without looking in will be more fluent in its movement.

Refrain from using any commands initially, and only intervene by gently rustling the bag if the dog cuts in towards the sheep, or looks in.

ABOVE: Entry into the training pen must be calm and controlled.

RIGHT: Dog should lie down at the threshold and once they are inside the pen.

Once he starts to cover the sheep, as he did when he worked outside the pen, after a couple of circles double back and prepare to stop him, only giving a command when you visibly notice him coming to a halt – he must be thinking about stopping when you give the 'Stop' command.

The Silent Approach

Working without verbal interference allows the dog to learn through experience. Dogs need time, not instruction at this stage, to assimilate and process information, and the silent approach has the following advantages:

- It ensures calmness in the training process, and will inspire confidence in both sheep and dog. Sometimes verbal commands can serve to excite your dog, depending how the command is delivered.
- It will give you greater time to think and predict the movements of the dog and the sheep.
- It will make you less tired, and give you greater focus on the task in hand.
- It will enable the dog to focus on your physical presence, and to read your body language without his equilibrium being disrupted by your voice.
- You will make fewer mistakes.

Spot – his face is averted as he runs through, signalling he is calm and confident.

- Your dog will learn naturally, at his own pace.
- Silence ensures that undue pressure is not placed on a dog, particularly if he is tired, anxious or sensitive, or all three.

There will be times when the sheep may be put under too much pressure and will run towards the fence or the edge of the pen so as to avoid the dog. Slowly move the dog, still on a long line, towards them, ensuring that it does not make any sudden movements towards them or they will get startled and run to another corner. Keeping the dog on the side of the fence, move closer to the sheep until a gap appears. Your dog may attempt to avoid going into the corner and try to double back, feeling vulnerable, so be careful not to be too harsh. If the dog is calm then allow him to run through the gap, but only when he averts his head away from the sheep towards the fence. This will ensure that you get a better flank, and it will also avoid the dog gripping.

Once the dog has gone round the sheep, you can repeat this exercise until he is confident enough to go through on his own. Once your dog runs the fence you must ensure that you do not stand in the way of the sheep, and should move backwards and out of the way, or even better, follow the dog round so that the sheep can move towards the centre of the pen. Once the dog gains in confidence he will be happier to force his way between the sheep and the fence and prise them away. It is quite common that as the dog goes through the gap, if the end ewe is slow to move, he will nip (a gentle bite without hanging on); however, don't make an issue of this, because it is more important that the dog grows in confidence, and with this, the need to grip or nip will decline. If your dog is very keen, ask him to stop frequently and to make small movements towards the gap between the sheep and fence so that he learns to nurse the sheep away from the fence, rather than bulldoze them.

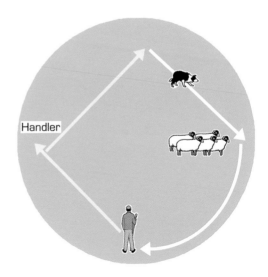

Send the dog through the gap, and follow close behind for moral support.

As with all exercises, it is important that you teach your dog to move the sheep away from the fence from both sides, as invariably dogs will always favour one side to the other. Once this element of training has been overcome, then often success in other areas will follow rapidly.

It is far easier to work with a dog inside a pen, as the long line is within reach, whereas if the dog is out of the pen he can be difficult to catch, as every time you move he will automatically move to the point of balance.

You will also find that your dog will respond better to stop commands whilst in the pen, because of your close proximity to him. Whenever you give a stop command to your dog, you must ensure that the command is taken first time, and if it is ignored then you either block any movement from the dog, or walk towards him until he lies down. It is crucial, however, that once the dog does lie down you do not, as a matter of routine, continue to walk towards him. If you do struggle to stop your dog, then don't worry, but just wait for him to tire. The stop is not the 'be all and end all' that it is some-

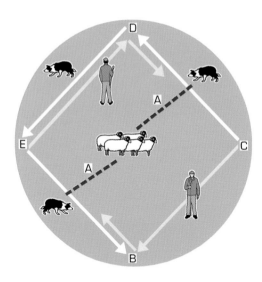

The dog flanks towards the handler. Give a recall command followed by a flank command; avoid eye contact.

times made out to be, in the early stages. You can focus on this more intently later on.

If you are confident that he will stay down, you can once more take up a position behind the sheep and continue. If you feel that your dog will move once you take the pressure off, then you must maintain your position in front of the sheep and stand facing the dog.

Only in rare circumstances would you actually ask a dog to lie down, and when it obliges continue to walk towards it, thereby applying extra pressure. This would be when the dog has resisted several commands and needs the point bringing home to it. You would maintain an upright stance in front of it, and repeat the stop command. Some dogs need a lot of pressure to persuade them to lie down, and with this type of dog you must be careful not to release the pressure too quickly, otherwise they will start to perceive the release of pressure as a sign that they can move. When you do finally walk back to repeat the exercise, remember to repeat the stop command so your dog does not perceive your silence as a licence to continue.

Another occasion when it might be appropriate to move towards your dog whilst it is lying down, is if it has flanked too close to the sheep. By walking purposefully towards the dog, it will move towards the fence. As soon as your dog starts to move out or away from the sheep, leave him to continue on the flank. There is nothing to be achieved by stopping him, and continuity is by far the better option.

Once your dog starts to flank correctly, at the correct distance from the sheep, inside the pen – that is, following the line of the fence – you can start to alter your movement from the square movement (*see* diagram on p. 114). Thus rather than following your dog round from position B to C, then C to D and finally D to E, you can remain at position B. As your dog flanks round, move to position E and meet the dog coming towards you. As you meet the dog face on, give him a flank command and he should continue to flank. Avoid giving him eye contact or he might stop and double back. You should also keep moving and head for position D.

When you move from B to E you will start to notice that the sheep will move slightly towards

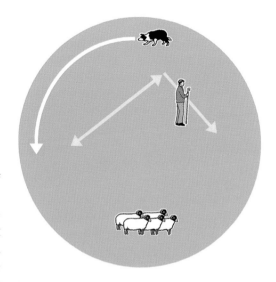

Move backwards out of the way as the dog comes towards you. Avoid eye contact.

position B to find protection behind you from the dog. The opposite will apply when you change direction.

If necessary, when you meet the dog coming towards you, give a recall command immediately followed by a flank command, to prevent your dog stopping and running back in the opposite direction. Another useful tip is to move backwards and out of the way as the dog comes towards you (*see* diagram on p. 120). This will serve two purposes: it will prevent the dog from cutting in between you and the sheep; and it will be less threatening to your dog and provide it with more room to flank (this is withdrawal of pressure).

The above exercise is particularly useful when your dog is cutting in on parts of the flank. It is not always necessary to use the square movement, as sometimes the voice alone is enough.

Skye is happy to flank past me as there is no eye contact or pressure.

CHAPTER 11

BROADENING YOUR DOG'S EXPERIENCE

TRAINING OUTSIDE THE PEN

Once you progress the training and move out of the pen, it is all the more important that you remember and repeat the same processes that you applied inside the pen, so that there is consistency at all stages. Once your dog recognizes that it is following the same principles as when it was inside the pen, it will settle very quickly into a routine. And although you will have more space, you should nevertheless start the session at roughly the same distance as previously, and gradually increase the distance at which you work.

Just because you are working out of the pen, with greater freedom for your dog and sheep, do not become preoccupied with the 'Down' command. I have seen many handlers become embroiled in a battle to get their dogs down, in vain, and this has merely served to make the dog's flank either too wide or too far. Once the owner has adopted a more silent and conservative approach, the dog has reverted to working far more smoothly and under greater control, without any interference. When your dog is ready he will lie down in good time.

Many handlers also compromise continuity for the sake of proving to the dog that they are the boss. If you bide your time and let your dog work, as long as he is not cutting in or gripping, enjoy the silence and let him carry on. Just use the square movements discussed previously to

keep the dog from cutting in. If you do notice your dog looking in or cutting in, just shout or growl or give a quick 'Hey!' command to dissuade him from coming in – however, keep these to a bare minimum. If he turns his head out again, allow him to continue flanking.

Consolidating Work in the Pen

Now that you are training outside the pen, try and consolidate the work you did inside the pen, so that your dog has some consistency. It is also important to keep commands to a bare minimum, just as you did earlier, and just allow the dog a chance to assimilate the bigger picture. You can consolidate the balancing process and start to move backwards, allowing your dog to bring the sheep to you. By walking backwards in a straight line and then changing direction gradually, your dog will have to use its instincts to naturally cover (balance) the sheep and continue to bring them to you. Your dog might try to flank, and you can block any movements past the 'quarter past' or 'quarter to'

Guiding Principle

Silence will allow you the opportunity to admire the poetry in your dog's movement and style of working.

ABOVE: *Mac making full eye contact, signalling his intention to come in.*

BELOW: *Spot keeps out, but glances with his eyes thereby applying less pressure.*

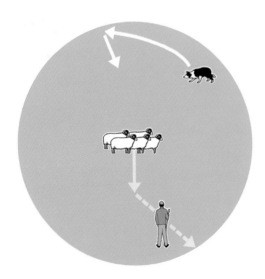

ABOVE: During a fetch create an angle. The sheep will follow, forcing the dog to balance to continue bringing them.

BELOW: The dog is blocked from running towards or past the handler.

positions, or ask him to lie down if he presses on too quickly. You might even want to raise your hands to block him.

As your dog settles into working in a bigger field, you can graduate to extending the outruns (larger flanks) by asking him to lie down and then pushing the sheep a lot further away than before, in the opposite direction. As soon as the sheep move far enough from the dog, walk back until you are 90 degrees from the sheep and dog. Ensure you are the same distance as you want your dog to be from the sheep. Stand still, face the direction that you want the dog to flank, and wait. As soon as you face the sheep your dog will become excited and might anticipate the flank command.

Prior to sending your dog, repeat the stop command, and only when your dog takes its eyes off the sheep should you then give a flank command. This will ensure that the flank and also the first movement is not a tight one, and does not upset the sheep. If your dog starts the flank by moving towards the sheep, ask him to stop and repeat the previous stage. If your dog is

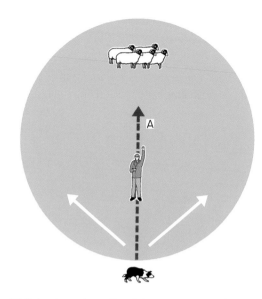

Walk backwards on line A to prevent your dog from anticipating the outrun.

Whichever direction you face whilst working with your dog, you should imagine you are working in a circular pen, where one half is your responsibility, and the other half is your dog's. If your dog attempts to flank into your half, stop or block him, unless he was invited in. Once your dog comes into your half of the circle by running past you, remain on the inner side and walk past him, swapping places with him. You will now be in his half of the imaginary circle, and he will be in yours.

Once the dog realizes that the pattern of training is as described in the following exercise, he will be happy to lie down and wait for you to move the sheep.

- Lie the dog down.
- Push the sheep away from the dog for about fifteen to twenty metres, increasing this distance as the dog improves.
- Move backwards in a straight line from where you left the sheep, i.e. 90 degrees from the dog and sheep.
- Ask the dog to flank.

extremely keen, then it is a good idea, even when he starts to flank correctly, to stop him as soon as he starts, and flank him again; this is so he can empty his head of any preconceptions. Even when I am competing with young dogs at nursery trials I will do this, as I would sooner lose a point or two at the start than risk a poor outrun and lift.

Before sending your dog, if he won't stand or remain in the down position, then position yourself to the point of balance, so that he doesn't know whether to go left or right (*see* diagram above).The point of balance is a straight line from the dog to the sheep. When you reach the correct position, about twenty metres or so away from the dog, move to one side and send the dog to the other. Imagine a fifteen- to twenty-metre ring round the sheep, and do not let your dog come inside this. Remember if the dog enters this imaginary ring, then as training progresses you can ask him to lie down and move the sheep or the dog out of the ring, in order to continue with flank training.

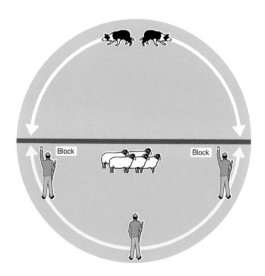

Don't allow your dog to flank towards you or in front of you. Blocking him will teach him to balance.

The dog is blocked on its left-hand flank from running to or past the handler.

- Move in the opposite direction to the dog, or follow closely behind depending on how the dog is working.
- If the dog flanks well, take the opportunity to walk backwards and allow the dog to bring the sheep towards you a short distance (a short fetch).
- When you are ready to stop your dog, move to one side, then give a stop command, so the dog appears to be past the point of balance and able to see you better. You also might need to take a step or two towards him.
- Alternatively, keep the dog flanking in the same direction by repeating the flank command, to then move past you. This is a good trust-building exercise, because in early training dogs will be hesitant to go past you in case you stop them. Avoid making eye contact with the dog.

Repeat the above exercise two or three times, and call your dog away from the sheep. This can quite often be a battle of wills, because although you wish to stop the dog from working, it will nevertheless want to continue. The best way is to ask the dog to lie down at the end of his flank, and then move towards him holding out your hand and clicking your fingers, to take

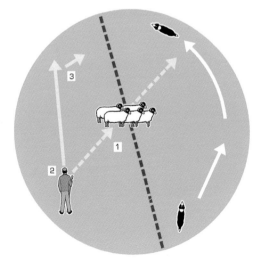

After moving sheep, handler and dog move in the opposite direction and meet at the top.

his mind off the sheep. Whilst he watches your hands and tries to work out why you are clicking, you will have caught up with him or the long line. Continue to repeat the 'Down' or 'Stand' command, and when you reach the dog, give him a stroke either on his side or his chest, not his head.

Whilst walking towards your dog, decide early whether to stop as you reach the long line and stand on it, or whether to continue all the way to your dog. If you do the latter, avoid eye contact, as this will put undue pressure on him; this will be less threatening to a young dog and will give him confidence. Take the line and, giving a 'That'll do' command, walk away in a casual manner.

If your dog wants to walk in front of you, allow him to do so, releasing the line, and when he reaches a position far enough away from you to your left or right side, ask him to lie down. Repeat this command, and leave him as you did before when you first commenced the exercise, and repeat the whole process once

Dog and handler must both be past the sheep before the handler delivers the stop command.

more. Repeating the above exercise four or five times in a row will serve to improve your dog's recall: he will come to realize that recalls provide continuity.

Stop the dog once you and he are past the sheep.

If you are dealing with a dog that is passive resistant, recalls can be difficult to achieve; the dog will sometimes lock out on you and freeze on the spot and refuse to move, particularly when you apply too much pressure. It will resist any pressure and not respond to you, will avoid eye contact with you, become confused and refuse flatly to move from the spot, in the hope that you will give up. In such cases, there is no point whatsoever in applying more pressure or losing your temper. Any form of training that is done in anger is totally counter productive. Rather, soften your voice and ask your dog to come with you. Move out of the ten- to fifteen-metre diameter limit and start again.

THE CONCEPT OF OPPOSITES

In the above case you are applying the concept of opposites – if one thing fails, try the opposite: for example, if you have tried to be hard, then try a softer approach, and vice versa. In some cases you might have first to try the firm approach, then when you get a slight response or reaction, follow up with a gentler command.

The concept of opposites is quite simple. Whenever you are faced with a problem, you will attempt to solve it from a human perspective because that is what you are. However, your dog is not human so why expect human psychology to work? I have found that when dealing with dog psychology, sometimes it is better to try the opposite in order to achieve success. Of course with any given problem area, your human logic will tell you that the opposite cannot work; however, in reality it does, and I have countless times experienced success. Some of the opposites you might like to try out are shown below.

Tip

Remember that in some of the cases shown in the table below, the methods that have failed may at some point also be the answer to your problems.

Failure to recognize a passive resistant dog may result in too much pressure being placed on it, and ultimately this could lead to the dog becoming aggressive, especially if it is physically handled around the collar area. If the dog is pressed in this manner it will gently bite the handler, but be aware that if aggression is met with yet more aggression by the handler, then a more severe bite may result. If you use your

Methods tried so far and failed	Opposites methods to try
Shouting	Whisper
Verbal command	Silence or non-verbal command
Soft whistle	Hard whistle
Tight lead	Loose lead
Stop the dog	Let them continue
Pressure on	Pressure off
Calling the dog past the handler	Sending the dog away from the handler
Working in a small paddock	Working in a training pen
Handler stationary	Handler mobile
Small number of sheep	Bigger flock

hands in any way other than positively, your dog will become hand shy, and its conditioned response to any hand will be an aggressive one. Some dogs might even 'pretend' nip – make biting movements in the air to persuade the handler to back off.

Where passive resistant dogs go to ground and won't move, avoid walking up to them and applying yet more pressure, because this will only serve to keep them down. Just walk away from the sheep and start again. The secret is to keep the dog moving and prevent it from going to ground or locking out.

There are many issues that will crop up whilst working inside and outside a training pen. To enable your dog to flow, you must constantly be on the move, not just so that the sheep can take up a position in the centre of the pen or field, but also to keep the dog moving. And remember, in order to keep your dog moving, the sheep must also be kept flowing; however, as stated before you must be careful not to cross the imaginary line between the sheep and the dog otherwise he will either stop, or change direction and run in the opposite direction. A dog will become easily conditioned to your movements and will anticipate them, and only by blocking him, verbally or non verbally or both, will you persuade him otherwise.

FLANKING PAST THE HANDLER

One of the hardest things you will ever do in training is to persuade your dog to go against the movement of the sheep. First it will have to run towards you, and then continue to flank past you (assume that your dog will be running in an anti-clockwise direction, to the command 'Away').

The best way to teach this is to ensure that your dog lies down when asked to. Then walk towards him, holding out your hand and continuing to repeat the 'Down' command in order to distract him. Then whilst moving towards your dog in a clockwise direction, give the command 'That'll do' when you are a couple of metres away from him, and encourage him to run towards you. If he takes the command and starts to move in your direction, then break your eye contact with him as you turn away from him, and quickly give the 'Away' flank command. Soon your dog will come to realize that the 'That'll do' command does not stop him from working, rather it is a means of continuing with the flank. By breaking your eye contact with your dog at just the right time you will also remove the risk that the recall command will lead to the dog stopping work. Another useful tip is to move backwards as the dog comes towards you: this will prevent him from cutting in between you and the sheep, and it will be less threatening to your dog and provide him with more room to flank (this is withdrawal of pressure).

If, however, you call your dog and he fails to respond, or alternatively tries to flank in the opposite direction to you, move sideways into the point of balance, between the dog and sheep, and your dog should stop. However, you will have to move swiftly and accurately, because any error will allow the dog to continue flanking. This time give a more forceful command and insist that your dog comes towards you. Remember that the command is

---

Tips

- If you find yourself standing still for more than a split second, this will lead to your dog cutting in on his flanks.
- If you find yourself running, you probably didn't move soon enough and you will upset the sheep, causing your dog to run faster.

not an invitation, it is an instruction, and refusal is not an option that your dog should consider. If, however, your dog ignores you and flanks in the opposite direction, just accept this minor setback and try again later.

When you are faced with adverse or difficult training scenarios it is far better that you stay calm and break the task into smaller, more achievable units, because this will take the pressure off your dog and make you less frustrated.

Always bear in mind that the long line and pressure techniques (including eye contact) must never be abused, or any trust you may have built up with your dog will quickly disappear. Furthermore, there is always the risk that any harsh or inappropriate behaviour on your part may come to be associated with any object or tool you use, such as a stick, crook or long line. Your dog may develop a conditioned response to that particular object, which when encountered may lead to him resisting you, running away from you, or flanking very wide.

TEACHING A DOG TO BALANCE

Saying that you are going to teach your Border Collie to balance is really a contradiction in terms, as most already balance naturally. Some handlers place a lot of emphasis on precision far too early, and can't wait to start using the 'Away' and 'Comebye' commands, or are ruthless in insisting their dogs lie down at the wrong time. Sometimes allowing a dog to continue or to find its own way is far better than feeding it constant commands. A dog that is allowed to develop its own abilities will pay you back countless times when you start to enter the bigger trials, where it can't either see or hear you very well.

A dog will want to bring sheep to you far more naturally and instinctively than take sheep away from you. The best time to teach the balancing and lift elements is when the sheep and dog are in the training pen. Once your dog starts to flank to its right, apply the square movement discussed before, and at the point where you would normally double back and stop your dog, continue to walk in the opposite direction towards your dog. Your dog will either continue running towards you, if it disregards your role in the partnership, or it will change direction and flank in the opposite direction. Once you have done this a few times you can test out whether your dog has started to balance, by allowing it to complete a half circle before changing direction. If your dog is flanking properly he will change direction as soon as you do, or very soon after, when he becomes aware that you have changed.

Once you have reached this stage you can move on to the next. Start just as you did before and allow your dog to complete a circle or a little more. At the point where your dog is furthest from the sheep and behind them, rather than doubling back to stop the dog, drift away and keep moving away (backwards) from the sheep for a few metres and then stop. As you move backwards the sheep will take up the space you have now created for them, and as you stop the sheep will also stop, causing the dog to come to a halt too. This will give the dog time to analyse the situation and to realize that the sheep need a little pressure to move them. By putting your dog in this situation you are forcing it to develop its own understanding about how much pressure is needed to lift the sheep (*see* diagram on p. 131).

Once the dog has settled, start to ease the pressure off the sheep by moving backwards slowly. Your dog may well start to move automatically and walk towards the sheep. Continue to walk backwards, avoiding any excitement or commands. Your dog might try and flank to move or even dart at the sheep. Watch his face and expression very carefully, and greet every change with a stop command, to avoid disturbing the flow of the sheep. Before you reach the

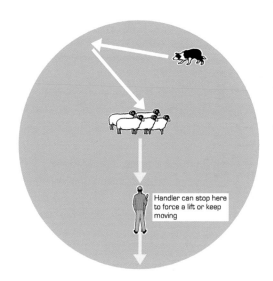

Handler can stop here to force a lift or keep moving

When your dog gives plenty of room at the end of the outrun, move backwards to enable a good lift and fetch.

end of the pen, stop your dog and start to turn slowly. Once the dog and sheep are at 90 degrees to you, ask the dog to flank, and stop him if he attempts to cut in. He may well flank naturally to balance the sheep without a command, and this is far better than having to give commands. If they flow round, then continue to walk round the pen, occasionally creating an angle, as above, to teach the dog to flank naturally and to balance. Remember that if at any point you are next to, or very near to the sheep, you most definitely will be in the wrong position and this will cause the sheep to move sideways.

Once the dog moves out of the pen, apply the same method, except that you can now use bigger distances – though keep an eye on the dog and make sure that he does not cut in or upset the sheep. Ask him to stop, and block any movement towards the sheep by placing yourself between them. By walking towards your dog with purpose, or by banging a stick on the ground, you will persuade him to turn out or to look away. As he does so, continue to

walk towards him and he will flank in the opposite direction to you. Then continue with the exercise as before.

INTRODUCING COMMANDS

The time to introduce commands is when your dog instinctively starts to flank correctly, giving good room to the sheep all the way round in both directions. Normally you should give a command to start the dog off, and repeat it when the dog either starts to slow down or stops in the wrong place, before it has covered all the sheep. It is also a good idea to concentrate on one side first, and then the other, rather than alternating, as the latter method will only serve to confuse the dog.

The only command you should repeat is the 'Lie down' command once the dog lies down, in order to prevent it from getting back up again. If you give only a single 'Lie down' command and go silent while you move into position, your dog will misconstrue your silence as permission to move. Usually it will either move towards the sheep, or it will flank in the opposite direction to you and balance. Some people use the command 'Stay' to keep the dog in place, but this should not be necessary as 'Down' means 'Stay down'.

Consistency of commands is crucial, as is tone of command. There is no point saying 'Down' once and changing to 'Lie down' later. In most cases your dogs will only react to the first syllable anyway. You must also emphasize each word in exactly the same way each time. The same is true for whistle commands. Some people – and I, too, have been guilty of this in the past – can develop a habit of changing the tone of a flank whistle, especially when the dog ignores the first whistle. This is caused by frustration or anger that the first command was ignored. You have to learn to stay calm and focused, and to use the same tone for each command, every time.

Tips

- If your dog flanks well, then trust him to flank on his own by moving in the opposite direction to him as he flanks, thereby meeting him as he passes the sheep.
- If your dog cuts in on the flank or does not flow round, you will be able to correct this behaviour by frequently stopping him, and using the 'square' flanking method. Closely follow the line between the dog and sheep, thereby putting gentle pressure on your dog not only to keep moving but also to flank properly. This is also useful when your dog refuses to flank in a particular direction.

Remember, your body position is a great tool in communicating with the dog which direction you want him to flank. So when you have completed a right flank and then wish your dog to do a left flank, stop him, cross the line between the dog and sheep, and turn in the direction you want to send the dog. Only once you are facing in the correct direction should you then give a left flank command.

Another way of improving flanks is to proceed as follows:

- Leave the dog by following the line between the dog and the sheep. This will ensure that your dog does not move or require regular stop commands, because you are at the point of balance and are therefore not signifying to the dog which direction he will be running in.
- Stop about twenty metres from the sheep, then cross the line on the opposite side to the one you want to send the dog.
- Send the dog on a short gather. If he cuts in, give a gruff command to deflect him, or

use the bag tool. If he continues to cut in, stop him and walk towards him showing your disapproval verbally, then resend him.

- As soon as your dog kicks out and flanks correctly, stop, glance at the sheep and move away from them. As they see the dog coming round they will take up the extra space you have created, thereby making more room for the dog to flow round.
- Ensure your dog does not cut in at any point.
- Allow your dog to move past the point of turn, and you can either allow a short fetch or continue to flank round.
- Before starting another flank you must ensure that you move backwards to a position which is 90 degrees from the sheep and dog and at least the same distance from the sheep as the dog is from the sheep. Do not move towards the dog, just walk straight back.
- Then when you are in a line that is behind the dog, face the direction you want the dog to flank and give the flank command.
- Once again only use flanking commands at the start of the flank, or if the dog slows or hesitates. Always keep the dog flowing round, and anticipate any hesitation. Remember, if the dog hesitates, walk towards him and insist that he flanks.

The secret to achieving a good flank is to ensure movement on your part, and to move away from the sheep as soon as you observe the dog flanking properly. By creating extra space for the sheep to move into, the dog will put less pressure on them when it arrives at the end of the gather.

Eventually as the dog comes to know the 'Away' and Comebye' commands, it might be worth testing this out by giving the commands whilst the dog is on the move. So for example if the dog is flanking to the right, without stopping it, give the left flank.

THE LIFT

The lift occurs at the end of the outrun when a dog moves carefully on to the sheep, and moves them calmly towards the handler in as straight a line as possible. As mentioned before, training a dog to lift sheep should be a quite natural process at the end of a flank or outrun, especially when you stand close to and in front of the sheep, blocking their forward movement. However, if the dog is too hard he must be taught to slow down on the lift by giving frequent stop commands.

In some cases teaching a dog to lift sheep correctly might be better done outside a pen, particularly if the dog is keen to keep moving on to the sheep at the end of the outrun. The reason for this is that your dog will have more room, as will the sheep, who will feel less threatened.

Some dogs are line dogs and move in a straight line, rather than flanking from side to side whilst working sheep, and these can be difficult to flank over a satisfactory distance: when given the flank command they will only move a few metres on the given side, rather than covering all the sheep and continuing to flank past them to the 'quarter to' or 'quarter past' positions. To correct this problem you need two things: a large field and a large flock of sheep.

A large field means the dog can give the sheep plenty of room, all the way round. Please note that this exercise is done at the end of the outrun, so you will be a fair distance from your dog, unless you move towards the sheep in anticipation of a mistake. Don't just stop the dog once it has moved past the last ewe, but keep it moving in a circle, so that it does not become conditioned to stopping behind the sheep. Note that the dog must maintain an equal distance from the sheep all the way round. Most dogs will favour one side and run wider on that side, but will come in on the less favoured side. If this

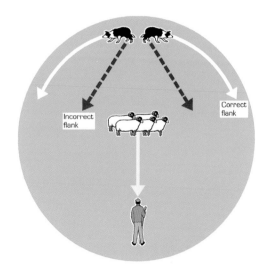

The dog should give equal room on each side on the flanks, whether fetching or driving.

happens, stop them quickly and move either towards them or in line, as appropriate. Your presence will push them out further. Once the dog starts the flank correctly, move back to your original position so your dog has room to complete a good flank, unhindered by you (*see* diagram above).

The larger the flock of sheep, the better the flank you will achieve with your dog, as it has more ground to cover on the flank. Your dog will feel less pressured with more sheep, as it will understand your reasoning far better than when you ask for a big flank with only a handful of sheep. If you do not have access to a large flock it is a matter of priority that you find a willing farmer who will let you use his sheep, because if the work you provide your dog is real and not contrived, your dog will be more open to change.

THE FETCH

As your dog's outrun starts to progress, there is a real temptation to stand back and allow him to

ABOVE: *Walk backwards when your dog gives good room on the lift.*

BELOW: *Bigger flocks allow for greater fluency and wider flanks.*

bring the sheep to you. Indeed, when you observe significant progress in your dog, it is all too easy to stand back and admire the results of your hard work. But remember, your hard work only ends when your dog ceases to make mistakes, which is never. You should always train with a critical eye, and if you are satisfied with a particular aspect of training, then you should question why.

There is nothing fundamentally wrong with allowing a dog to fetch sheep to you, at the end of an outrun, if your dog can balance correctly. However, a young dog generally finds it difficult to break contact with the sheep, therefore eliminating this problem should take priority.

One of the hardest tasks to achieve at a nursery trial is when you run on young hoggs. They rarely wait for a dog to reach them on an outrun, and take off. In such circumstances it is far better if your dog is taught to continue running on their outrun until they head the sheep; a good balancing dog will do this naturally and without command. Once the dog has lifted the sheep, it is highly likely that the sheep will want to continue or 'ware' sideways in the direction they were running before, and in this case it is more practical to have a dog that has been taught to flank wide, after lifting the sheep, rather than bringing the sheep to the handler, directly from the point of balance (*see* diagram above).

When working with flighty sheep, it is quite rare for the dog to be able to walk behind them at a steady pace. A more likely scenario is that a straight fetch will be achieved through good, wide flanking movements, rather than the dog walking behind the sheep. To achieve this level of control on the trial field you must first put it into practice at home. Every time you stop your dog at the end of the outrun, allow him to lift the sheep, then stop him and let the sheep drift towards you. You may need to give repeated stop commands to halt any movement forwards.

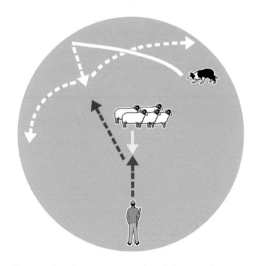

Ensure the dog runs past the sheep on the outrun. Allow a short lift before asking it to flank either left or right.

Once the dog accepts that he will not be allowed to walk on to the sheep, turn yourself in the direction that you want your dog to flank, and give a flank command. Your dog may resist this command and continue to walk forwards, in which case stop him and give another flank command. Even if he takes the flank, he may still stop short further on. Again, stop any movement forwards and make him flank until he reaches the 'quarter to' or 'quarter past' position. Continue to practise sending the dog from 'quarter past' to 'quarter to' and vice versa, without stopping at the point of balance (*see* diagram on p. 136).

Only when you feel that your dog is flanking correctly on one command and starting to become fluent should you allow him to stop at the point of balance and walk on to the sheep. Remember, when your dog is supposed to be flanking and instead he walks on, this will cause the sheep to deviate from the straight line; if this happens at a trial you will lose points. The same problem while trying to pen sheep can make the difference between a clean pen and points lost.

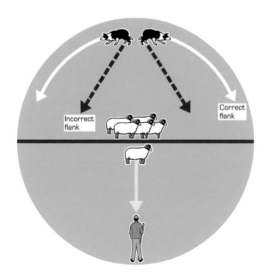

Flanking the dog from side to side without stopping it will prevent the sheep being upset, and improve the flanks.

There is far too much made about the point of balance at sheepdog trials, with references being made to the dog 'stopping at 12 o'clock'. I much prefer to see a dog that is prepared to run past the sheep so that none are left behind, rather than a dog that stops ten metres short and lifts the sheep in totally the wrong direction, away from the handler. In my mind the clock analogy only works if you do not assume that the handler stands still facing in one direction only.

Imagine the sheep moving to, say, the 'ten to' clock position: the handler will adjust his/her position so that they are facing the sheep at 'ten to'. The 12 o'clock now also moves to the 'ten to' position (*see* diagram on the right).

A lift that results from an over-flank on the outrun will bring the sheep towards the handler, whereas a dog stopping short or under-flank ultimately takes the sheep away from the handler, particularly if it does not balance well.

Don't always teach your dog to fetch in a straight line, otherwise it will not be flexible enough to go where you want it to at the end of the outrun. Practise fetching diagonally, or even straight across the field. Remember, anything that is different in your training regime will excite not just you, but your dog also. Training must always be a labour of love, and should not be seen as a chore.

Also it is not always practical for the dog to stop directly behind the sheep, particularly if the gates are offset or diagonal. Remember, farm gates aren't always set conveniently in a straight line. Furthermore, a dog that is taught to go past the point of balance will be of greater use, particularly if sheep are scattered over a large area and are unsighted by the dog. Just as you should learn to trust your dog, your dog needs to learn to trust you. Once your dog goes past the point of balance and can see the reason behind your insistence to continue on the outrun, it will not resist further commands with the same vigour.

It is also a good idea to sometimes leave your dog at the end of the outrun to lift the sheep without a command, and to fetch the sheep to you without a command. There are far too many directional commands given to dogs at trials,

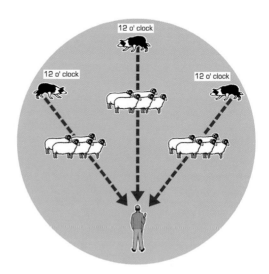

If the sheep drift to the left of the handler the 12 o'clock position moves to the left of the handler, and vice versa.

ABOVE: Skye flanking naturally to cover the sheep instinctively.

BELOW: The point of balance is reached by the dog when the sheep come in a straight line towards the handler.

which in my mind are not necessary. The added advantage of teaching a dog to feel for the type of sheep they are working is when you send them on a blind outrun. There is no sight better than when you send your dog up a hill and he disappears over the brow, and not only finds the sheep, but lifts them correctly, and proceeds to bring them to you without a whistle or verbal command.

Wide Flanks

I have heard many debates on the merits of a wide flank or square flanks. This is where a dog, whilst flanking the sheep, moves horizontally away from the sheep thereby not putting them under pressure. For example, if the sheep are tucked in a corner when the dog flanks, at the point at which it passes the sheep, it will continue to follow the line of the fence, hedge or wall. It will also turn its head away from the sheep, as opposed to looking in and leaving the boundary too early.

Regarding the finished article, I prefer a dog that flanks squarely but will also walk on to sheep, or come in when asked, and come in without hesitation. A dog that takes off too much pressure without the ability to apply it also, can be frustrating to work, as the sheep will learn to take advantage of this. Of course, some naturally wide-running dogs fall into this category, and this problem can be worked on through confidence-building exercises. This type of dog gives more respect to sheep, and such dogs are less jerky in their movements. They will prise sheep away from a particular spot, whereas strong dogs will cause them to bolt. It is a matter of personal preference which style you prefer and how patient you are.

Dogs that are not wide flankers and are strong require a greater degree of obedience. However, this isn't a guarantee that they will not upset the sheep, especially if they are lying down and being asked constantly to get up. Wide flankers

can stay on their feet as they don't put the same degree of pressure on the sheep. Some weak dogs with a lot of eye will also be able to get away with tighter, more direct flanks without upsetting the sheep; however, they tend to be a lot more precise and careful in their style of work, and consequently use up more time.

Many young dogs will flank better on one side than another, and if this is the case, like any other exercise, it will be necessary to devote time to correcting this problem. It is, however, crucial that the timing of such exercises is taken into consideration. As with any exercise, if too much pressure is placed on a young dog, the mistakes made can be irretrievable. It is natural for young dogs to push on to sheep and to hurry them. This is perfectly acceptable whilst you are trying to teach the basics, although you should still let them know if you object to something they do, without making a big issue out of it.

It is also worth bearing in mind that there will be many occasions when you might actually *want* a dog that moves towards the sheep in a direct and forthright manner. Only when all the basics have been taught and you have come to understand the type of dog you have, should you attempt to polish a dog off for sheepdog trials, and this includes square flanks.

When you train a young dog it is easy to label it too quickly, in my opinion, as a hard or a strong dog. I prefer to reserve judgement until I start to polish a dog and refine its training for trials. I have also seen many handlers label their dogs incorrectly. For example, a dog can be strong in type without being hard. Hard, for me, is when a dog resists change introduced by the handler in certain aspects of training, whereas a strong dog can be easy to train but have a forceful way with sheep – it commands respect from sheep. Unfortunately, when you first start to train a dog it is not always obvious whether it is hard or strong, due to its exuberance, and it is only once it has learnt the basics that the picture slowly starts to unfold.

Spot gives good distance on the flank and looks away from the sheep.

A mature dog will have progressed through the various stages of training and will have grown to understand your handling style and to cope with different levels of pressure, and therefore will not sulk or become anxious when you attempt to push it out further. Also the right time to give alternate flanking commands is when the dog is on the move, in order to broaden its experience. A dog that can think whilst it is on the move will have a greater turn of speed than one that has to lie down first before receiving a flanking command.

Teaching Square Flanks

It is necessary to have square flanks in order to move the sheep in a particular direction, and in many situations you need to flank a dog without the sheep moving forwards, for example at the pen or when trying to negotiate an obstacle. I also prefer a dog that runs freely, as the sheep are not placed under any stress. Ultimately the ideal is to teach your dog to run wide, and also to come in when asked to do so.

The way to achieve square flanks is to stop the dog on the flanks as soon as it goes wrong, which very often is at the very onset. You should therefore follow up a flank command immediately with a stop command. Always take care never to block the dog's vision of the sheep, and walk parallel to the dog. Look closely at the dog's face, and whenever it either looks away or turns its head away from the sheep, give the flank command. This will have the effect of making the dog turn out better from the very beginning. Don't worry about positioning or setting up the dog physically, as this can only serve to make a young dog more nervous or anxious. It is far better to keep the exercise low key and merely stop the dog if it goes wrong. As soon as the dog realizes that you counter every movement inwards or every glance at the sheep by blocking that movement, it will start to run wide.

If your dog actually makes a move towards the sheep, it is important not just to block this movement, but also to take a step or two towards the dog, and to physically put pressure on him to stop. Whenever you do this it is essential that as soon as the dog stops, you do too, otherwise the dog will feel threatened. Depending on the severity of the mistake, you can either release the pressure by moving back, or stop in your tracks and maintain full eye contact and a square-on position. At the same time you should be repeating the stop command, firmly and positively, as an instruction, not a request.

Also remembering the lesson earlier, don't allow the dog to stop at the point of balance,

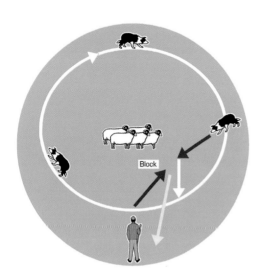

As the dog cuts in, move in line, give a gruff command and move back quickly to allow the flank to continue in front.

rather keep him moving, sometimes in a full circle. Also whilst he is moving do not allow him any glances at the sheep – if he happens to look in, just give a growl or stop him. Remember, however, that continuity is crucial to young dogs, and if it is not necessary to stop the dog, then don't. It is also during this phase of training that you should consider asking the dog to flank past you, as described earlier. Remember that when a dog flanks past you it must leave good distance between you and also the sheep.

It is very easy to put too much pressure on a young dog, and you must be sensitive to your dog's state of mind. If you notice that he does not wish to flank towards you or runs too wide, a subtle whistle to call him in can pay dividends. You do not always have to apply pressure by moving towards your dog. You can achieve equally good flanks by moving parallel to your dog, or in its line of vision; you can reduce the level of pressure applied by avoiding direct eye contact with your dog.

It is just as crucial to have good flanks whilst driving as it is when fetching. To achieve this, follow the same process as described above. Stop your dog if it cuts in, and move in line with it. As it starts to flank, move backwards quickly, thereby giving it plenty of room to flank in front of you (*see* diagram on the left). If you fail to move back quickly or far enough you will cause it to be too close to the sheep. Alternatively your dog will flank behind you and the object of the exercise will have not been achieved.

This exercise requires impeccable timing, because if you do not move backwards in time your dog will not flank correctly, and will feel more pressure than is required. Some dogs can become sensitive to too much pressure, and other aspects of their work can also suffer.

THE OUTRUN

Teaching the outrun is merely an extension of the flanking exercise described earlier. Leave the

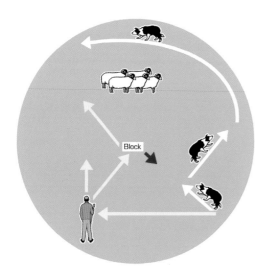

If your dog cuts in, move parallel or towards the dog making a gruff sound to dissuade it from coming in.

dog in the 'down' position further and further each time, and command it to run in the opposite direction to you. Before you allow your dog to progress to a bigger distance, it is important that any deviations towards the sheep whilst flanking are checked, by stopping the dog and moving toward it or sometimes parallel, and letting it know that it has made a mistake by giving a short growl or gruff command, or even a check whistle (a shorter version of the stop whistle). By continuing to move both sideways and in front of the dog, you are giving yourself extra time to correct any mistakes made by your dog. It will also ensure that you do not have to run after your dog and create further excitement (*see* diagram above).

Remember, once your dog completes the outrun you should continue to double back to a position which is past the sheep so the dog can see you clearly before you deliver the 'stop' command. You may allow him to lift the sheep, but thereafter take up a position between the dog and the sheep. Then facing the direction in which you wish to send the dog, ask him to

flank, and ensure the flank is completed correctly. Once this flank is complete you can practise either the same or the opposite flank. Alternatively, call your dog off the sheep and walk away in order to start another outrun/gather.

Extending the Outrun

By the time your dog is running up to a hundred metres to cover the sheep he is ready to start the outrun from a position nearer to you than before, but still not directly next to you. Rather than asking a dog to outrun from a position next to you, as you would at a trial, keep ten to twenty metres from him; this way, if he does happen to come in on his outrun at least you are better placed to apply pressure. Remember, pressure delivered from a distance has a greater impact than when you are close to your dog, or next to it.

Each time your dog comes in, move in line with it or towards it, depending on the severity of the mistake, and redirect it. If you pause for a while your dog will try and work out what it has done wrong, and will try and correct the error. Sometimes it is just as easy to push a dog out by verbal commands than physical pressure. Using the bag tool, as described earlier, will also be useful, though do not over use or abuse this. In some cases, if you pause long enough, your dog will flank correctly on its own, without redirection.

Whether you are teaching the outrun or flanking elements, maintain eye contact with the dog's face and look for telltale signs as to whether your its eyes convey intensity or resignation. If it is the latter, then sometimes it is far better to allow your dog to continue flanking, and reward his positive contribution. Remember, for the dog, just as your putting pressure on him is the consequence of his breaking the rules, allowing him to continue is the greatest praise you can give.

By the time you progress to sending your dog from your feet it is still advisable, as an insurance policy, to send him on to his outrun only once he turns his head away from you, then immediately stop him. Wait for him to settle, and send him on his outrun again once he turns his head; this will ensure that any ideas he might have had of running in tight will be checked.

Some dogs that are of a very strong nature who can't wait to get on their outrun can become highly aroused by the fact that they are about to be sent on their outrun. If this high level of excitement is rewarded and the dog is allowed to gather the sheep, it is highly likely that either the dog will come in on the outrun or that when it arrives behind the sheep it will be impatient to lift them and will put too much pressure on them, causing them to bolt. With this type of dog it is far better to calm it down before allowing it to outrun, and to proceed in the following way:

- Set up the dog to run on the outrun, about two to six metres away from you. Note that restrictions at sheepdog trials apply, whereby the dog must be close to the handler or post before commencing the outrun.
- Give it a quiet 'Lie down' command, and wait. It will more than likely ignore the

Handler still, dog's tail carriage low and still, and ears flat – a great way to start an outrun.

command and continue to focus on, or eye up, the sheep.

- When the dog realizes that you are not yet allowing it to run, it will make eye contact with you.
- Expecting that you might give a flanking command, its body might twitch in antici-pation. Repeat the 'Lie down' command when it looks at you. Ensure that the dog does lie down, applying pressure if neces-sary by moving closer to it; however, stay calm.
- Leave the dog in the down position, and repeat the 'Down' command.
- If it stays calm, showing no further body twitches, allow it to run; otherwise tie it up and repeat the exercise later, as necessary. Alternatively, if you have other dogs with you, choose the calmest one and work that one.

If your problem is not with the outrun but with the lift element, then sometimes it is better to stop the dog early on its outrun, before it reaches the sheep. You can either stop it two or three times until it reaches the sheep, or ask it to over-flank past the sheep. It might be worth-while practising this element at close quarters by placing the sheep in a corner and getting the dog to lift them slowly by repeatedly asking him to stop, and 'nursing' the sheep out of the corner. Also, rather than allowing the dog to run out of the corner to head the sheep off, stop him in the corner and ask him to wait there. Allow the sheep to walk out calmly, and then either call your dog on, or allow him to lift the sheep quietly without a command. With luck your dog will show a bit of eye in lifting the sheep, rather than using his whole body.

Another way of dealing with dogs that are tight on the sheep at the end of the outrun is to keep them moving in a circle. This will open them out and break the conditioned response of always stopping behind the sheep at the end of the outrun. A dog that continues to run on his outrun until asked to stop is an absolute godsend.

Some dogs that are easily conditioned, or those that have very strong chase instincts, may be difficult to stop and redirect; they might also hit the sheep hard at the end of the outrun. This type of dog needs more time spending on consolidating the basics, and the slightest of glances inwards whilst outrunning needs to be checked either by stopping the dog or voicing your objection, depending on how serious you think the consequences might be. Also by vary-ing the outrun and walking out parallel to your dog, you will stop bad habits from forming, and stopping the dog in mid flow will be much easier. By changing the manner in which you do particular exercises, you will maintain greater control over your dog.

In some cases you might have to ensure that the distance your dog runs past the sheep on its outrun is greater than required and exaggerated, so that it gives more room to the sheep, enabling a better lift.

Once a dog starts to outrun over a couple of hundred metres it is better not to set it up for the outrun, by turning it away from the sheep. This way when you deliver the flank command, you will know instantly how well it knows that command. If it does take the command correctly, make sure that the flank is also correct and the dog does not cut in at any point. The less your dog relies on physical or non-verbal cues from you, the more confident you can be that the verbal command has been consolidated.

Dogs with Strong 'Eye'

Dogs with strong 'eye' have a tendency to freeze as soon as they come into contact with sheep that are stationary or moving slowly, especially towards them. Rather than using their physique or posture or movements to cause the sheep to

Spot, eyes up on the lift, enough to calm the sheep.

move, they rely on the power of their eye to persuade sheep to move. There may also be a certain lack of confidence that serves to slow the dog down. Sheep that are very flighty respond well to this type of dog, as the eyes have a way of drawing the sheep to the dog and instilling trust. Dogs with 'eye' have a low chase instinct when it comes to sheep, and are therefore more inclined to hold back and be patient; this is why they can get so much closer to sheep and hold them, thus making it easier for a farmer to catch a sheep, should he need to. My own dog Fly has this great ability, and can walk tediously slowly up to sheep and sniff or even lick them on the nose. If, however, one walked up to her, then this is totally different as far as she is concerned, implying a threat, and she curls her top lip just to warn it off. At trials, however, Fly (now retired) was boringly methodical and the least pleasurable to compete of all the dogs I have ever worked.

Living with a dog with strong 'eye' undoubtedly brings mixed fortunes, and 'eye' is not something you can get rid of. You can, however, learn to manage the problems, and alter your handling style to compensate for the amount of 'eye' the dog has.

When teaching the outrun to a dog with a lot of eye, which might stop short of the packet of sheep, as soon as it starts to slow down you must connect with it, either by voice or whistle, and let it know that slowing down is not acceptable. It needs to learn and recognize that it is doing something wrong and making a mistake. When you observe a dog slowing down unnecessarily, at any point, give an extra flanking command or make a gruff sound. If it doesn't listen, walk purposefully towards it, and this might persuade it to continue flanking without command. If it doesn't automatically start to move, give it a flank command and insist that it flanks. Some dogs might respond better to a verbal command than a whistle, so it is better to use the former. Some dogs that are passive resistant or nervous may go into lockdown mode (*see* Chapter 4).

As with all expected mistakes, it is far better to deal with a thought, rather than wait for the actual behaviour to manifest itself. So if you think that your dog is about to do something wrong, based on previous experience, then correct it before it goes on to make that mistake – in the same way that if you saw a child about to run out on to the road you wouldn't wait until it was on the road before you acted.

If your dog refuses to flank, change the way in which you are delivering the command, and soften up. If necessary move your dog out of the zone – the distance between the sheep and dog – that is causing it to 'eye' or lock up.

Once you break the contact between sheep and dog the flank command will be taken more readily. Do not allow this eyeing up to go uncorrected, because you will pay for this fault time and time again.

The following exercise will help with dogs that 'eye' sheep:

▨ Place yourself alongside a wall or hedge and ask your dog to bring the sheep to you. When they come to a standstill the dog will be provoked into using its eye.
▨ As soon as this happens, move to one side, thereby releasing the pressure, and allow the sheep to run away from you.
▨ Stop the dog momentarily to allow the excitement to build up, and then release it by using a specific command – not a flanking command – such as a shushing sound or any word that serves to invoke excitement in your dog.

Repeat this exercise a few times and your dog will start to anticipate your actions as well as those of the sheep; in time it will come to associate the use of that command with its use of 'eye', and it will become excited on hearing it. In Fly's case the command that made her excited was a 'bleating' sound; other handlers use whooping sounds or even clapping. As an extension to this exercise you can stop the dog further back each time and walk the sheep to the wall or fence. Eventually you will be able to leave the sheep against the wall and walk away with your dog, then send him on a short gather.

As the dog gains in confidence you can extend the outrun further. The secret is to deliver the commands in the same way each time, which will, hopefully, invoke the same positive reaction in the dog. However, don't get complacent because you will need to repeat this exercise with different sheep and on different terrain to achieve the same level of success.

At trials, one of the first instances where dogs with strong 'eye' will come unstuck is with the lift. You can train to avoid this by extending the above exercise as follows: put the sheep in the corner of a field or against a gate, and walk your dog up to the boundary line. Using a long line may be of benefit as you can use it to move the dog at will if it gets stuck, though sometimes it is easier to have the dog on a shorter line or even baling twine looped through the collar, for easy release. Create a gap between the sheep and the gate or fence, and send the dog through. If you know your dog will stop short or hesitate, then take him with you and complete the manoeuvre together, whilst on a short line/twine.

Your dog will soon realize that stopping or eyeing-up is not an option, and that it will be made to run through and bring the sheep out of the corner. Running through the gap and coming out the other side to head the sheep will cause a huge adrenalin rush in your dog and provide lots of fun.

The following is an extension of the above exercise:

▨ Place the sheep in the corner of the field or gateway by moving them there yourself and keeping the dog back, about eight to ten metres away. If the dog is confident enough to walk on to the sheep, allow him to do so without having a lead attached. However, if he is in any way hesitant, or wants to flank, then attach him to a length of string or baler twine and walk to the sheep with purpose, giving the command 'This'.

- Continue moving until you cause the sheep to move, then turn and return to the starting position. Your dog will grow in confidence as you repeat this exercise, and will start to anticipate the sheep's reaction.

- To end the exercise, allow the dog to complete a flank between the sheep and the fence or hedge, and bring the sheep out into the field. Rather than getting the dog to fetch the sheep to you, position yourself and help the dog to bring the sheep out of the corner, once again moving with

purpose, as if power walking. Your dog will gain in confidence, and you should allow it to drive the sheep away with this renewed vigour.

- Call the dog off before it slows down, and repeat the exercise again.

Note that this exercise presupposes that your dog can already drive and flank correctly: allowing your dog to drive before you have achieved good flanks can be a formula for disaster. This exercise can be used not only if you have a dog with a lot of 'eye', but with any dog that lacks in confidence or self-belief.

This exercise will be useful whilst penning, and if a ewe turns or faces up to your dog. There is no sight better than when a dog stands up to

Mac running freely along the wall in order to prise the sheep away.

ABOVE: Dogs must be taught to maintain steady pace and pressure when sheep face up to them.

BELOW: Once the sheep turn and face the wall, repeat the exercise.

Head to head – both sheep and dog have to face their demons.

a facing ewe and moves towards it with authority and exerts its power, persuading the ewe to concede and move on.

Continuity will be the key to your success with dogs with eye. You should also refrain from asking the dog to lie down at the end of the outrun, but try and keep him on his feet and moving. As long as the sheep keep moving you will be able to avoid your dog eyeing up. Unfor-

tunately, you will merely be delaying or postponing the inevitable agony, as when the sheep reach the shedding ring. To prevent problems, keep yourself mobile, thereby preventing the sheep from settling. If you are lucky, an opportunity may well present itself to shed.

Once the shed is complete, again you should keep the sheep moving and make haste towards the pen. It is crucial that you keep them moving right into the mouth of the pen, because then at least you are in a position to help your dog. If, however, the sheep stop short of the pen, they will turn and face the dog, and this may well signal the end of your trial. At this juncture you will need to decide whether to use the array of exciting commands, such as 'Look', 'This', 'Take hold', or the shushing sound, and so on. Inevitably you will risk the chance of your dog gripping. If, however, you have done your homework well, your dog will have the extra push needed to successfully pen the sheep. If you don't pen the sheep, especially with a young dog, then don't worry. What you must never do is get angry and risk upsetting your dog, or he will not relish this situation and will switch off under the pressure.

Keeping the sheep mobile is the key to working with strongly 'eyed' dogs. I have seen many good runs come to an abrupt end once the sheep have worked out that the dog lacks in power. They reach a decision to 'work to rule', or would go on a 'go slow' and test the dog. I have also observed handlers being over cautious and stopping their dog once too often, causing the sheep to stop and graze. The key to working with this type of dog is pacing at the correct speed. Keeping a dog mobile will serve to make it think it has more power and give it self-belief, and with time your dog will develop the ability to cope with the heavier types of sheep.

Positioning the Sheep for an Outrun

When you first start to develop your outrun it is more advantageous to have the sheep away from the perimeter and towards the centre of the field, so that your dog learns to give plenty of room at the end of the outrun. However, as you develop the outrun and build the distance, it is far more useful to place the sheep, not in the centre, but rather at the end of the field, no matter how big the field is, as this will teach the dog to keep running until it finds its sheep. If the

---

Tips

- If you have a weak type of dog you should prioritize teaching your dog to pace positively.
- Secondly you should prioritize confidence-building exercises.
- Don't expect your dog to be pushy with heavy sheep too soon.

---

dog gets used to finding its sheep conveniently in the middle of the field, it will expect the very same when you take it to a trial, and this doesn't happen very often.

It is also a good idea to place the sheep right up against the boundary fence or wall, so that the dog has to force its way between the sheep and the boundary in order to lift them. A dog that can prise sheep off a boundary can make the difference between completing a run and retiring.

Blind Outruns

Before you go on to teach your dog to run out blind – when the sheep are out of sight – you should ensure that your dog is able to achieve all other basic elements correctly, namely outrun, lift and fetch. In addition your dog must have confidence in both you and its own ability, and you should be able to stop it anywhere on its outrun, not just at the end.

Rather than starting off with a big distance, start off with the sheep just out of sight and gradually increase the distance; this way, your dog will be better prepared and unlikely to make any drastic errors. If you keep on at your dog too much you will undo the good work you have already achieved and risk upsetting and confusing it. Prior to sending your dog there is no reason why you cannot show him where the

Sometimes a gap must be created.

sheep are, and then move to a position that is out of sight. This will minimize the instances of your having to stop your dog and giving frequent commands.

Another method is to place the sheep in position within sight, and send the dog on an easy 100 metre outrun. Then return the sheep to the same position and move 200 metres, then 300 metres, and so on until the sheep are totally out of sight. Even when the sheep are out of sight, I continue to increase the distance in the same manner until I run out of room. Of course, this will involve a lot of leg work; however, if you are blessed with owning a quad bike, then this exercise will not pose too many problems. This method of training is known as 'backward chaining', so the dog starts off with an easy task and builds to slightly harder ones each time, with the precise knowledge of where the sheep are. Once the dog has achieved a blind outrun confidently, you can then progress to moving

the sheep to a different position and test your dog yet further.

THE DRIVE

Some dogs are born with the ability to drive sheep away quite naturally and without hesitation, whilst others are very unsure and prefer to head the sheep in order to bring them back to the handler. As the instinct to bring sheep to the handler is stronger, in the Border Collie, than the instinct to drive them away, some dogs become very confused.

When teaching a dog to drive, timing is of the utmost importance, because a dog that is allowed to drive sheep away too early is effectively given the message that it is quite all right to walk on to sheep. This will not pose a problem as long as your dog flanks correctly and stops when asked. If, however, when you give a flank command, regardless of whether the dog is driving or fetching sheep, your dog moves on to the sheep and upsets them, it is definitely not the right time to teach your dog to drive. Many novice handlers are impatient and will allow a dog to drive sheep too early, only to find that this impacts on other aspects of training. Remember that a dog that takes sheep away from you brings a whole set of different problems to when it is bringing sheep to you. In many instances the terrain you work in can make it difficult to highlight whether your dog is making mistakes, and therefore to correct them.

It is best to achieve the outrun, lift and fetch elements correctly with your dog, as well as moving freely and positively, before attempting to teach the drive. No exercise should ever be contrived and false. Your dog must at all times see that there is a reason for moving sheep in a particular way or direction. Again, don't work with too many preconceptions or you will only be disappointed and your dog will sense the negativity, which in turn will affect performance.

The type of sheep you use to teach the drive is very important: they need to be free moving so that they do not slow down and cause the dog to become uncertain. On many occasions I have waited until I am in North Wales to teach this element, for three reasons: the sheep are naturally lighter and livelier; my dogs are keener because the sheep are new to them; the terrain is different.

Decide which part of the field the sheep naturally run to, as this will ensure continuity. However, if the sheep move too quickly the dog may be provoked into heading them. Before attempting to drive, send your dog on a short gather, ensuring that all elements are completed satisfactorily. Stop him at the point where you want the sheep to turn, ready for the drive. Ask him to flank past you as he would at a trial, then moving on the opposite side to your dog, start to walk on to the sheep. Ask your dog to walk on, parallel to you. Ensure that the sheep are moving before asking the dog to move. If you move with purpose you will cause the sheep to keep moving, and your dog should follow.

Free-flowing sheep are a must when teaching a dog to drive.

ABOVE: **Starting the drive: push the sheep first to get them moving, then allow the dog to begin driving.**

BELOW: **Stay within your dog's peripheral vision, and walk parallel to him.**

When dogs become confident driving, move behind them and cross to the opposite side.

If your dog starts to head the sheep, call him back into line with a recall or flank command and continue. At this stage you should merely assess how confident your dog is, how much natural ability he has, and whether he has a tendency to want to head the sheep. Alternatively, ask him to lie down for a moment, then turn and face the sheep yourself, and ask the dog once again on to the sheep. This way you will turn a flanking movement into a drive once more.

Slowly and gradually your dogs will gain confidence and start to move ahead of you. If they do so and are positive, hold back a little and move behind them, and continue to the opposite side so that you remain in the dog's peripheral vision. It is important that your dog is aware of your position, and it will move with confidence if it believes you are not far behind.

As your dog moves further and further away you can swap sides behind him so that he is practising the drive element from both the left and the right sides as he might at a trial. Don't worry about controlling the pace of the dog in the early stages: you can work on slowing him down later.

As with all exercises, rather than just practising a manoeuvre, get your dog to drive the sheep from one field to another so that it thinks it is doing a job for you and sees a purpose to the exercise. Some dogs don't like to take sheep from one field to another and often try and head them off, to prevent them from escaping; therefore once the sheep run into a different field, allow the dog to continue driving them before allowing them to disperse, then walk back out of the field with your dog, but not too far. You can then send him on a gather once more. By introducing these different elements early, when you come to polish your dog off later and entertain the blind outrun and shed, your dog will have been prepared for this: rather than being fazed by new or different elements, he will be excited by them.

Another exercise you can practise, particularly if your dog falls into the 'heading' category, is to drive along a fence or hedge. This will stop the dog wanting to head the sheep, particularly if he is on the hedge side and you are parallel to the dog. Once you reach the corner of the field ask your dog to flank tight between the hedge/fence and the sheep, to bring them out of the corner ensuring that they run the line of the fence and do not upset the sheep. There is nothing worse at a trial than achieving a perfect turn and then causing the sheep to scatter and break away from the line of the cross-drive. Again this is a task that has to be practised to give dogs confidence. You can now either go back along the same hedge, with the dog now on your opposite side, or continue along the next hedge.

Once your dog becomes a proficient driver, another element you can practise is to teach them to turn the sheep in front of you, rather than taking them past you. Many trials now incorporate a turn in front of the handler rather than behind in order to save time and make the field bigger.

Dogs that look back constantly at sheepdog trials or at home can be frustrating, as they are taking their eyes off the job. Apart from demonstrating a shortfall in their training, these dogs will also lose a lot of marks at sheepdog trials, for not concentrating on the task at hand and allowing the sheep to deviate off the straight line.

The secret to avoiding these problems is to be aware of your dog's state of mind. If whilst he is driving he suddenly slows down, this will be due to uncertainty, so pre-empt this by doing one of three things:

- If you are stationary, start to walk towards the dog, remaining in his vision, and move the sheep yourself.
- Give your dog the 'Look' command as you would prior to commencing work.
- If you are moving with your dog, ensure he can see you, and walk with greater purpose.

Refrain from calling your dog off from a drive position as you will encourage him to look back. Send him on a short gather, and call him off after that so he is already facing you.

The above points should prevent your dog turning round and looking for help and support. If, for whatever reason, your dog does start looking back at you, don't reinforce this by giving a command, otherwise you will be rewarding your dog for looking back, albeit inadvertently. Even giving eye contact to your dog can reward him for looking back. Walk as before and move the sheep yourself. As soon as your dog sees you moving towards the sheep positively, he will follow suit and do the same. As he turns on to the sheep, give the command 'Look' or make a 'shushing' sound and continue as before, as long as the sheep are moving away without slowing.

In the case where an older dog looks back at you occasionally, give a firm 'No' command or 'Look' to indicate that he has done something wrong. This will soon put him back on the right track.

As your training progresses and your dog starts to drive well, occasionally take the sheep towards a closed farm gate and ask him on to the sheep. Of course as soon as he/she enters their personal space they will come to an abrupt halt. You can now actively teach your dog to walk on to the sheep, to discover his hidden strength and the power of his eye. After a while release the pressure by opening the gate and continue to drive the sheep into the next field. Your dog will experience a huge sense of satisfaction. Repeating this element a few times will also give confidence to your dog.

CHAPTER 12

ADVANCED TRAINING FOR TRIALS AND FARMWORK

TEACHING YOUR DOG TO PACE CORRECTLY

Teaching a dog to pace is crucial when competing with your dogs at trials. It means the run can be completed in good time, at a steady pace, and with no stress being put on the sheep. Also it is far better for a judge to see a run that is smooth and consistent without the sheep speeding up and slowing down or even stopping.

Some dogs have a very natural pace with sheep, maintaining constant pressure throughout and holding their topline flat; others will push on too hard with a tendency to lift their head up – 'lolloping', as I call it. I much prefer the former type of dog, as they tend not to upset the sheep through erratic movement; the latter type of dog, with its constant change of pace as well as posture, can disrupt a good run if it goes unchecked. Aim at all times to have a workmanlike and practical run.

Dogs should be taught to lift their sheep correctly at the end of the outrun, and correct pace will ensure this. Some dogs that are too strong need to be asked to lie down before being immediately asked to walk on to the sheep; others can be trusted simply to slow down and walk on to the sheep.

I recall watching Sydney Price many times, whilst letting sheep out at trials, with his dogs coming in at the end of an outrun to be given a quiet check whistle, just to remind the dog to be careful. The dogs would slow down for a split second, turn on to the sheep in one movement and lift them very calmly, in the straightest of lines towards the fetch gates, with minimal commands. It was a joy to watch, a perfect example of practical shepherding with the dog working on its feet, holding a constant pace and saving time.

Teaching a dog to pace is not something I worry about until I am polishing off the dog for trials. In the early stages I prefer a dog that moves on to the sheep positively with confidence. If you knock the early enthusiasm shown by your dog you may come unstuck when faced with heavier sheep or older, stubborn ewes. Also this will cause your dog to become uncertain and hesitant, which in the context of a trial can consume a lot of time.

Whether dogs are competing at nursery, novice or open level, you should continue to emphasize this element of training as it will ensure that the dog doesn't become complacent or haphazard in its way of working with sheep. This is especially important where dogs perform a dual role, of helping you on the farm as well as competing in sheepdog trials.

Pacing involves a great deal of walking, both with the dog bringing the sheep to you and driving them away. Ask your dog to gather the sheep, and leave him to bring the sheep to you. Initially you will have to move swiftly backwards and in a straight line so that you can keep an eye on your dog. If you get any sudden changes in pace or movements by the dog, ask him to lie down before asking him on to the sheep again. Sometimes with a stronger type of dog you can use a stick held up in the air to remind him of your position and also to distract him. You can also give a check whistle to slow your dog down, rather than asking him to constantly lie down and risk upsetting the flow. Also, keeping this type of dog further back will give the sheep and you more time to manoeuvre.

Do not allow the sheep to settle and graze, and ensure continuity at all times. If you notice them slowing down, ask your dog to increase its pace slightly to keep them flowing. This will motivate your dog and give him great pleasure as well as confidence. Once the sheep have become trained to your movement they will follow you anywhere, and this will then enable you to dictate the pace at which you move. In some cases, however, the sheep may hassle you and move at you too quickly. Stop the dog and move in a forthright fashion towards the sheep with your arms out, and they will soon realize that you are not prepared to be hassled by them. Once they settle, call the dog on once again. Once the correct pace has been achieved with both dog and sheep, you can relax and walk normally facing the front. This will enable a quicker and better pace to be achieved.

This exercise requires the handler to be quite fit, as walking backwards places great strain on your calves and if your fitness is not up to scratch, your dog may well be working at the correct pace but you may hinder his attempts by allowing the sheep to catch up with you. To avoid this, when your dog flanks correctly and gives the sheep good distance, take the opportunity to move into position. By the time the dog completes the outrun you will be a good distance from the sheep ready to move backwards. This will buy you precious time and distance. Once your dog gets the idea and maintains a constant pace you may then walk

normally facing the front and occasionally glancing over your shoulder to check on the sheep and dog.

The distance you need to walk should be as realistic to a fetch at a sheepdog trial as possible. Once you reach the end, create a gradual angle and allow the dog to balance/flank naturally without a command. Correct any movements towards the sheep, and ensure that the flank is a good one before moving back up the field. Once you have practised the fetch element you can change over to moving/driving the sheep away from you. Initially you can start by standing parallel to the dog, but as it starts to flow you can manoeuvre yourself behind the dog and even move to the opposite side so that your dog can see you and feel your presence. By moving confidently you will inspire your dog to do the same. Sometimes if I have a dog that paces well and naturally I will pair it up with a youngster so that the youngster can learn from the old hand. The power of the pack is a very strong force and should not be underestimated.

A dog that can pace well will not only be a godsend whilst undertaking a fetch or drive element, but will also help you in the shed and pen by keeping the sheep calm. It is easy to disregard this type of training, but to my mind it remains one of the most important, and considerable time and effort should be devoted to it.

SHEDDING

Shedding or splitting sheep is the act of separating either two or more sheep from the rest of the flock and driving them away, or preventing them from joining the rest of the flock. This aspect of training probably causes the most debate above any other, as there are so many different areas to consider.

Teaching a dog to shed is normally one of the last elements of training to be tackled, once the dog is working under control, driving, has good recalls and is confident in its work. Teaching the

Power of the pack – dogs learn willingly from one another.

shed is also much easier when using a larger flock – say, of twenty or more sheep – simply because it is easier to make them split.

Teaching the Shed

- Start by asking the dog to walk up to the sheep until it comes to a standstill due to its proximity to the sheep. Then, working from left to right – with you on the left – give a 'Stand' command, and walk into the sheep and create a gap large enough for the dog to come through comfortably.
- Make eye contact with the dog and encourage it to come to you by clapping your hands to draw its attention to you.
- As the dog comes towards you, turn to the packet of sheep you want to shed, giving the command 'This', and walk towards them, moving forwards first and then diagonally to your right, leaving the dog slightly behind you.
- This will cause the sheep to move to your left, and as they do so, give a left flank command to your dog and it will willingly do this in order to cover the sheep. The dog should flank behind you and not in front just yet. By keeping the dog behind you it teaches him to flank properly.
- Some young dogs will try to head the sheep, just as they did when you first taught them to drive. Just stop them and call them back into line in order to drive the sheep away.
- Once the dog starts to drive the sheep forwards, swap places with him again –

ABOVE: Skye maintains a steady pace as she comes through, keeping the sheep calm.

BELOW: Perfect teamwork – moving to the right will cause the dog to take up the counter position to the left.

that is, move to your left diagonally, causing the sheep to move to your right, and ask the dog to flank behind you to the right.

- Repeat this zigzag or scissor movement, and proceed to drive the sheep a good distance away – about twenty to thirty metres or more – before asking the dog to return for the other packet and join the two packets together. To avoid confusion some handlers use the 'Turn back' command to rejoin the sheep after shedding, as opposed to a 'Look back' command for a double gather. However, don't become predictable, and vary the distance. Occasionally take the packet of sheep out of the field and put them in another field, and continue to drive them in that field. Then send the dog for the second packet and continue to work with that packet.

- If the dog comes through too quickly or harasses the sheep at any point just ask him to lie down for a few seconds before continuing in order to prevent the sheep from becoming upset.

- Once the dog is happy to drive the sheep away you can revert to standing still and let him do the work.

Shedding at Sheepdog Trials

At a trial, shedding is a more precise art than at home on the farm, where you just want to get the job done. Of course the sheep at home will know what you are trying to do, unlike at a trial, having been handled before and used to being shepherded with a dog.

As with all elements of work, success in the shedding ring will depend on how you have

Sheepwork is a partnership – handler and dog both move to the left to stop the sheep.

treated the sheep whilst negotiating the trials course. Before the shed starts the approach into the shedding ring is vital. Many handlers do not pay enough attention to the line from the cross-drive into the shedding ring, either because they are relieved at hitting the final obstacle or because they are thinking about the shed. Of course not all trials have shedding rings, although it is always a good idea to pretend that there is a ring, as I'm sure the judges do, as this will help you to stay focused and keep the work tidy.

The movements you and your dog need to make in order to shed sheep are exactly the same as when you were teaching your dog to balance the sheep. I have observed many able-bodied handlers stand in one spot on a blistering hot day and proceed to let the dog run round and round the shedding ring, trying to hold the

sheep to the handler. By the time they move to the pen the dog has had enough and is exhausted, not to mention working too far from the sheep. If your early training went smoothly your dog will come to recognize your movement and positioning, and will accept your commands willingly.

It is just as much the handler's role to hold the sheep to the dog as the reverse – if the sheep attempt to leave the ring it is just as easy for you to move parallel to them and hold them to the dog. At least this way you can control your own movements and pace exactly. Also with some types of sheep it is better for a handler to move the sheep towards the dog, than for the dog to be asked to bring the sheep to the handler. If you are in too much of a hurry to achieve a shed, you will only succeed in upsetting the sheep, causing them either to bunch up or to leave the ring altogether. Just think back to how many times you have seen people at a trial, who try and force the sheep or hold them against their will, causing them to try even harder to make their escape.

Depending on the type of sheep you have, if they are easy to shed then it won't matter too much whether they are facing you or your dog. However, where sheep are stubborn and bunching together, it might be better to leave the dog lying down and walk the sheep towards him so they are facing him. This way the dog can eye the sheep and hold them whilst you apply pressure on some of them to move, thereby creating an opportunity to shed the sheep you want.

Preparing to Shed

Once the sheep have negotiated the cross-drive hurdle you should always glance at the centre of the shedding ring, to judge the line and bring them in a straight line into the centre. Before proceeding to the shedding ring ensure that the first sheep, at least, is in the ring. If you have made an error, depending on how serious it was and what advantage might have been gained, either points would be deducted or some judges would even choose to disqualify. If you have watched several previous runs you will have a good idea of how you need to negotiate the shed, and will have considered the following points:

Patience is a real virtue in the shedding ring.

- You should have a good idea which direction the sheep want to run in. Always place the dog on this side as he will be far quicker than you should the sheep make a sudden dart.
- You should have decided which of your ewes is the leader, as this one will move first in the above direction.
- Do the sheep run to the handlers for safety from the dog? If so, you may need to put pressure on the sheep as soon as they enter the ring.
- Do the sheep need to be allowed to settle in the ring for you to gain their trust before attempting any manoeuvre?

The harder you try to shed sheep the harder the task becomes. The best handlers I have observed have the following in common:

- They wait patiently for an opportunity to arise and don't rush. They also don't worry about running out of time. It is better to achieve a perfect shed and run out of time than to jeopardize points for the shed and pen. I have heard of judges who will take off more than ten points from the shed element, say fifteen, and leave five for the pen.
- They allow the dog to play its part. If you can get your dog close enough, his eyes will mesmerize particular sheep, causing them to stand still, whilst you apply gentle pressure on the rest to move away.
- They shepherd the sheep in the ring, giving them plenty of room to feel safe and secure.
- The dog comes in calmly and turns gently on to the sheep before taking control of them. The dog, and not the handler, walks on to the sheep first, which are then held from the rest. Although it is not a requirement to drive sheep away, many handlers will nevertheless do this to demonstrate control.

Skye is allowed to discover her own strengths, while I stand still and give support.

- Where appropriate – with five sheep and not four – the dog comes in and takes the last two sheep, not the front two, as this shows greater strength of character.
- Once the shed is complete the sheep are reunited, in the ring if practical. Although this is no longer a requirement at trials, it still looks more professional. Finally, they are moved into a position that will bring them in the best line towards the pen.

A great deal is made about dogs coming in on a shed 'at the speed of light' or 'like a bullet', which is fine if they don't upset their sheep. Once sheep have been upset in the shedding ring it can be a difficult task to calm them down again in order to pen them. It is far better to have a dog coming in steadily and turning on to the correct sheep calmly and taking control of them quietly.

Common Shedding Problems

Dogs Not Coming Through

If you have been too hard or unfair whilst training your dog, the shed element is where your dog is most likely to pay you back. Dogs are easily conditioned and come to recognize the shed element; some even relish the opportunity to shed sheep away due to a primitive, predatory instinct to separate and kill sheep. If your dog makes a mistake, the last thing you should do is call it to you and chastise it. Also, should you place too much pressure on your dog it will refuse to come to you and will run very wide. At trials, in particular, your dog will sense that you are tense and will avoid coming to you at all costs. The best thing to do is to address your recall problems first, and also stop practising the shed long enough for your dog to forget.

Dogs Anticipating the Shed and Coming Through Uninvited

Once your dog is confident at shedding, practis-

ing the shed and driving the sheep away in the same way each time can become a formula for disaster. The ideal situation is that the dog only comes in and drives the sheep away when it is instructed to do so, but many dogs will anticipate coming through as soon as a gap develops. To avoid this problem occurring it is far better to practise the international-type shed, where the unwanted or uncollared sheep are shed off between handler and dog, with the dog only coming in to 'turn back' the wanted or collared sheep from leaving the ring.

Another point worth bearing in mind is that the handler is not permitted to 'manoeuvre for cuts', whereby he manoeuvres all the collared sheep to one end and then sheds off the rest in one go. This way the dog does not come through every time, and learns to be patient and play the waiting game. The added advantage of this method is that your dog can also practise singling in this way by cutting off individual sheep, until only one is left.

One recent rule change that is worth mentioning is that once shedding is complete the handler may push the unwanted sheep away with the dog to prevent them from interfering with penning. Previously, able handlers would chase the sheep away, which looked unsightly – after all, why have a dog and chase the sheep yourself?

Hesitant Dogs with Strong Eye or Lacking in Confidence

Dogs with strong 'eye' will often not come through and take control of the sheep positively or quickly, as they are too busy eyeing up and waiting for a reaction. The scissor movement discussed earlier is by far the best way to teach the shed, as you move the sheep first, which causes the dog to react.

More Man than Dog

Shedding is a partnership, and the handler should take great care not to jump in too quickly

Skye plays the waiting game while I concentrate on doing the maths.

to make a gap. Use the collie's inbred ability and 'eye' to achieve the task, and once the dog comes through, allow it to move on to the sheep first and to drive them away. Provide help only if required, for example if you think a ewe might try to join up with the shed sheep.

Many judges prefer to see the dog taking control of the sheep, with minimal or no help from the handler; however, national rules do not specify that the handler cannot help. My own preference is to let the dog do the work, as it is not always possible to know what a judge will be looking for. Also if you get into the habit of helping your dog to drive the sheep away, you may well come unstuck whilst undertaking the 'single' element. This is discussed further later.

THE DOUBLE GATHER OR TURN BACK

The 'Look back' exercise is probably the last training element I teach, and I am probably more cautious about this element than any other. This is because some dogs become far too easily conditioned, and there are so many set routines that can be confused. At the very onset of your sheepdog training you will have taught the 'Look' command. This command should also be used on every training session, or contact with sheep. The 'Look back' is simply an extension of this command.

There are four methods that can be used when teaching the 'Look back', and which ones you use will depend on your personal circumstance.

Method One

The following method is appropriate when you have only a few sheep to train with:

- Walk into a field where there are some sheep, and as you walk towards them give the command 'Look'. Continue to walk right up to the sheep, occasionally repeating the same command.
- Turn and walk away from the sheep. Your dog will be bemused you didn't let him work and will not want to leave. As you walk away he will probably turn and look back at the sheep. As he does this, give and repeat the command 'Look back'.
- As he faces the sheep, ask him to stand momentarily, and give an appropriate flank command. As he starts to run, repeat the 'Look back' command once or twice, depending on how far the dog is from you.
- Allow the dog to bring the sheep to you a short distance, then allow them to drift past you and walk to the dog and continue walking, asking the dog to come away with you. Once again as your dog looks back give the command and follow the above procedure.
- Soon your dog will start to anticipate your actions and respond to the 'Look back' command. Once your dog learns the commands, start to increase the distance so that he learns gradually, without becoming confused. Once you send your dog on the second gather, remember to ensure that the outrun, lift and fetch are all correct.

Method Two

If you have a large flock, the following method can be less contrived and far more enjoyable for both handler and dog:

- Ask your dog to gather the flock of sheep and fetch them back to you.
- Then shed the sheep, roughly half and half, and ask the dog to bring one packet of sheep to you.
- Once you are forty to fifty metres or so away from the second packet of sheep, stop your dog by giving four 'stop' whistles close together. These whistles will become associated with the 'Look back' unless you give four 'stop' whistles in any other situation.
- Then leaving the dog there, walk towards it, and face and look in the direction of the second packet of sheep.
- Once the dog sees you walking towards it, it is very likely that it will turn and look behind to see why you are walking in its direction. Once it turns and looks at the second packet, give the 'Look back' command; as it turns, ask it to stand momentarily before sending it on the gather, giving the 'Look back' command once more, followed by the flank command.
- Once your dog is starting on the second gather you can repeat the 'Look back' command once and maybe twice, depending on how far he is from you. Mistiming a command will cause the dog to turn back and look at you.
- If your dog doesn't look back naturally, continue walking until your dog does look back. Some dogs wait until the handler is either parallel with them or just past them before turning and looking.
- Once the second fetch is complete you can change direction and get the dog to fetch the sheep in the direction they have just come from. You do not need to allow the two packets to join up just yet.
- Once you have walked far enough, repeat the process and do another double gather.

Mac flanks to his left ready for turn-back and gather to the right.

Method Three

If you *don't* have a large enough flock, then the following method will give you a decent chance of succeeding in teaching the 'Look back':

▨ Send your dog on a normal outrun and allow him to lift the sheep and fetch them a short distance.

▨ Call him back to you a short distance, and then give the 'Look back' command or whistle, and again the odds are very high that your dog will automatically turn back and look. As he turns back give the command again, followed by the 'Stand' command.

▨ Wait a short while before sending the dog on another gather.

▨ When you call your dog off the sheep, the next time you can send it to gather on a different side to the first. Pay attention to any mistakes your dog might make on the gather.

▨ Increase the distance gradually, as with the previous method.

The advantage of this method is that the dog

knows exactly where it has to go, so it is easy for young dogs to adapt.

Method Four

If you have access to a lot of land and sheep, then an opportunity will often present itself to you when you are shepherding, for example where the sheep are in two different lots or more; you can then use any of the methods described above, or a combination of them, and provide the most realistic education and experience for your dog. When a dog learns a new task 'on the job', so to speak, then its age is not so important as it might be with some of the more contrived or manufactured methods.

With the first two methods the sheep may well try at some point to rejoin the other group, and this is a great exercise to test out how much power your dog has by preventing them from joining up.

Unless you desperately need to, don't practise this element too often, as overdoing this might cause your dog to go back at a trial, particularly if it has seen a second packet in a nearby field. Also ensure that any whistle commands you introduce cannot be easily confused with any other whistle, such as a flank whistle.

Over time you can extend this exercise by hiding a packet of sheep, providing you have enough land, and sending your dog to double gather on a blind outrun. This will be the ultimate test for your dog as it will need to be obedient, to stop when asked to, and to take any redirection without hesitation and without cutting in. This type of exercise is not for the young dog and requires tremendous strength of character – although I have seen many exceptions.

Be warned that attempting this type of training can cause tremendous confusion in your dog, and lead to problems in other parts of his work, such as the lift and fetch, or even the outrun.

Tip

When doing a turn-back at a trial, be careful not to deliver the flank command until your dog is still or is moving in that direction, otherwise he may spin round and turn on to the first packet of sheep. In some cases if the dog is heading in the right direction, don't give any extra whistles unless he hesitates or appears unsure.

PENNING

Penning sheep is one of the most crucial elements at a sheepdog trial, for many reasons. If members of the public are present there is extra pressure on the handler to pen the sheep, as it is an expectation arising from the television programme 'One Man and His Dog'.

Some trials have a shed or single element after the pen, so if you cannot pen the sheep you will instantly lose twenty points. In some cases sheep have to be put through a Maltese cross – where gates are placed in a cross shape with four openings – prior to penning, and again if this element is not achieved, points for the pen will be lost.

Many experienced handlers do not practise penning, choosing instead either to put the sheep into a corner of a field, or to use natural obstacles in the field as markers, placing the sheep between them. The advantage of moving sheep into a corner is that it stops the dog from over-flanking, and also teaches it to slow down, thereby putting less pressure on the sheep. Greater emphasis is placed on the precise movement of the dog in relation to the sheep. Flanks need to be clean, yet short, as well as slow. Stops need to be precise, and movements from the down into a stand, or vice versa, need to be gradual and smooth. Of course a dog that stays on its feet is less likely to disrupt sheep

Swaledale ewes happy to accept an old hand.

because it avoids the jerky movement of lying down and getting up. This type of dog is a great help, as an upright posture is more assertive and challenging than a low position, close to the ground.

Dogs also need experience of coming in close to sheep and not feeling threatened by them, or threatening them. This is possible when you have regular access to sheep pens – although many farmers will tell you that working dogs for lengthy periods in pens is not always advantageous because they can become highly charged when in such close proximity to sheep. They also become accustomed to hustling them and getting the job done quickly, because time takes precedence over precision. In my own experience it is always a good idea to work dogs in a close and confined area if only to broaden their horizon, but save this type of intensive work until after competing at a trial, rather than before, where possible.

As with other aspects of work, penning sheep is a partnership and the handler has a big part to play. It is trial etiquette to regroup the sheep following a shedding exercise before proceeding to the pen, leaving the dog to bring the sheep to the pen. Depending on which line the sheep take towards the pen, it may be prudent to wait before opening the pen. If at a trial you have observed handlers struggling to pen sheep, it might be worth trying a different tactic, on the presumption that 'nothing ventured is nothing gained'. Some handlers leave it quite late before opening the pen gate, usually when the leading ewe makes eye contact with the gate, opening it gently to invite the sheep in. Others prefer to be ready, and open the pen gate as soon as they reach it. My preference changes according to the type of sheep I have. If I am working with very flighty sheep I sometimes choose to open the gate once the sheep have made eye contact with the pen, so that they can see the opening clearly.

Once the sheep have moved successfully into the pen it is essential that you do not close the gate on to the last ewe and push it with the gate: this would be considered a gross error, and once again either points would be deducted or you would be disqualified. The same result would ensue if you let go of the rope whilst penning sheep.

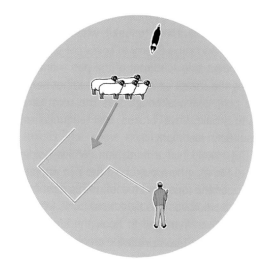

Avoid running to the pen, and bring the sheep as close to the pen mouth without stopping.

Penning at Trials

It is uncanny how many times the sheep at sheepdog trials will be quite content to stand in front of the pen yet refuse to go in. Yet when the whistle blows, signifying that the time is up, they will walk straight in. If you find yourself in such a situation it is useful to remember that you need to maintain the utmost calm. Just as your dog has the ability to distinguish between different smells, the sheep too will sense if there is tension, created by you and reflected in your dog's behaviour.

The manner in which you move the sheep towards the pen is crucial. Sheep should be taken gently and carefully towards the pen mouth without stopping and with just the right amount of pressure (*see* diagram above). If you have had trouble from a particular ewe whilst taking the sheep around the course, then it will need watching carefully. Awareness is the key: if it happens to be in the right position it might lead the others straight into the pen; on the other hand it might slip down the side of the pen, and you need to anticipate this. Avoid any unnecessary stick waving because threatening

sheep hardly ever leads to a successful pen, and can send them scattering, as well as prevent them from coming near you.

Remember also the 'pressure on' and 'off' techniques. If you or your dog is putting too much pressure on the sheep they will turn and face you, rather than turn away from you and walk into the pen. Nevertheless it is far better that you put the pressure on the sheep rather than on your dog, because at least you can withdraw from the sheep and start again.

Successful Pen: Harold Loates and Skerry

I have never forgotten Harold Loates (South Leverton) attempting the pen at Tilton Sheepdog Trials 1997 with his bitch Skerry, whom my dog was named after. After the cross-drive gate the sheep were heading for an open gateway, where the spent sheep were grazing. Harold reached the pen seconds before the sheep, and as he untied the rope the sheep were about to pass him. Skerry was nowhere near, as Harold had

putting their own stamp on the proceedings. (Information courtesy Wyn Edwards.)

There is sometimes a conflict with judges failing to interpret rules correctly. Sometimes there is also a conflict between rules and working in a practical way. Ultimately it is the handlers who are the most practical and workmanlike who are most successful.

As with the shed exercise, time is always a factor to be considered, and many handlers carry a stopwatch so they can gauge when to take a risk. Generally speaking, rushing sheep will more often than not upset them and nothing will have been gained. If it is to be your day, whatever actions you take will work. Sometimes Lady Luck plays a big part in determining the results, but 90 per cent of time the experienced shepherd who has spent time watching and studying sheep, and who practises each element meticulously, will win the day.

THE SINGLE

Many open trials do not incorporate the 'single' element (shedding off one ewe from the rest) due to time constraints. The 'single' normally comes after the sheep have been penned, although where only three sheep are used at trials then handlers are sometimes required to single before proceeding to the pen, as an alternative to the shed.

Teaching a dog to single is in some respects

Skye ready and confident to go it alone and take charge.

an extension of the shed, although it is not recommended that you teach shedding and singling at the same time. Allow the dog to become familiar with the shed element first, and only when the dog is confident as well as proficient at this should you attempt the single. The dog must also be confident driving sheep. Once your dog becomes proficient at coming through when called, at holding sheep and letting sheep go, you can go back to practising the international shed as described earlier, which teaches both shedding and singling simultaneously.

The approach to the 'single' exercise is the same as the shed, however, greater patience is called for. Sheep have to be calm and feel secure to split up from the rest, although a leading ewe can sometimes provide an early opportunity, provided you can stop the rest from following. You should also position your dog and teach it to walk on to the sheep slowly, so that it learns to eye a single ewe. By getting the ewe to focus on the dog, you may well be able to draw the rest of the packet away from it. Remember, it is the dog that should come in to single the ewe from the rest, and handlers should refrain from lungeing in themselves. Once the ewe has been singled you can use the same scissor movement mentioned in the 'shedding' section to give the dog confidence; however, bear in mind that at a trial held under national rules the handler is not permitted to assist the dog in driving the sheep away. It is also a requirement that prior to the single, the handler will proceed to the shedding ring, leaving the dog to bring the sheep from the pen into the ring.

At a trial, watch the sheep as they enter the ring and see where the ewe that you wish to single is positioned (sometimes ewes to be singled have a collar on). If it is the leading ewe, simply by walking parallel to it you might be able to persuade it to walk a little faster, whilst you can apply gentle pressure on the rest by moving towards them slightly to hold them

back, thereby creating a gap. Once the dog comes through, allow it to take control. Some ewes are very clever at using the handler to escape from, or hide from the dog, therefore if you move out of the way the ewe is left with no place to hide – although be careful that you do not appear to be helping the dog to drive the ewe away. Doing this may also prevent your dog coming in and gripping the ewe.

Use of the commands 'This' and 'Look' will help immensely as the dog comes in to single: not only will they give it confidence, but they will energize your dog into taking control. Remember, if you have used these words/commands in training whilst walking with your dog and driving the sheep away, the commands will later, at a trial, serve to reinforce the fact

---

Tips

- Achieving the above level of understanding from your dog takes time and great patience. Avoid chastising your dog or putting him under too much pressure by shouting at him. If your dog has poor recalls then avoid this exercise and focus on recall training.
- Don't practise this element too much as your dog may start to anticipate a single rather than a shed at trials.
- Some handlers actually tell the dog what type of shed element they will be doing by stating either 'one' or 'two' before proceeding to do the exercise.
- Where the single follows the pen, ensure that your dog does not go to the back of the pen before you have shut the pen gate, as the sheep may run out of the ring thereby costing you a point or two.
- Avoid exaggerated jumping in or cutting movements, as points will be deducted. Quiet control is called for.

ABOVE: If you need help, just give me a sign.

BELOW: I've warned you before, don't be so hard on the youngsters!

that you are there and giving confidence, even if you are not walking with the dog.

PRESSURE AND SHEEP

Pressure is critical when working with sheep, not only in achieving certain elements, but in protecting young puppies from bossy old ewes or rams that are protective of themselves and their flock.

During the shed element you can manoeuvre sheep into the correct position by applying and withdrawing pressure. If the sheep learn that you place greater pressure on them than the dog they will be less likely to hassle you and run to you for cover. They will also move more willingly towards the dog, giving it the opportunity to use 'eye' to hold one or more ewes in position for the handler, to effectively shed the required number of sheep.

A dog with strong 'eye' will need to maintain constant pressure to keep the sheep moving, because if the sheep are allowed to come to a stop and graze they will be armed with enough information to turn and stand on the dog, or run in any direction they wish. Some young dogs can find it difficult to drive sheep away with the same level of confidence and at the same pace as they did during a fetch, because with a drive element they are moving the sheep away from their source of support, namely you. It is a good idea to walk parallel to them and help them drive the sheep away. Alternatively, allow your dog to work with another dog that is much bolder and more confident, and the young dog will learn from the 'master'. Many older and more experienced dogs are very tuned into pressure. I have noticed when using older dogs to train youngsters that they will keep out of the way until they feel the youngster needs help – for example, if the sheep are about to run off or stand up to the pup.

During the pen element, pressure has to be just right. Your dog should be allowed to bring

Portrait of a Successful Handler – Aled Owen

Aled Owen describes in his own words what drives him towards success.

Aled Owen – Welshman with nerves of steel.

I have always been very competitive and determined ever since I was young. I remember winning the Senior Sheep Shearing Championship of the British Isles and Ireland on 24 July 1986, like it was yesterday.

I started training dogs when I was seventeen in Bala with the ATB Instructor, Garnett Jones, and won my first trial when I was eighteen with Jess. Alan Jones (Pontllyfni) was the first to come over and shake my hand. I came to know him very well and he would invite me to his farm on Sundays to train with him. It was never a short visit and often I would be there for six hours or more. Sometimes it got dark and we would still be out running dogs by torchlight. Alan was the most

natural handler I have ever seen and he had a way with dogs that no one else did. What's more, if he had a bad run he would flick his tie up to his face and was able to laugh about it. He didn't take things too seriously.

Eddie Humphries (Trefnant) was another handler that influenced me greatly. He never criticized my handling but his comments were always very constructive. I learnt a lot from him.

Regarding a preference for dogs or bitches, I have had and seen some really good bitches. However, I have never been very lucky with them. They have been difficult to breed from as they have come into season in the middle of the trial calendar. Previously bitches in season were not permitted to run until late in the day so it was far simpler to run dogs. Jess was a really good bitch and made the Welsh team in 1980 and 1982.

Penyfed, my farm, is 750ft above sea level with the land rising to 1,700ft. I have rough grazing and pasture land, and although the biggest single field I have is only 10 acres, I can send the dogs up to half a mile away through four different fields. Most of the sheep are out of sight and the dogs have to have the ability not only to find their sheep but also to be able to bring them down, negotiating the gates. I like dogs with natural ability, good temperament and confirmation. I am not particularly worried about colours or coat types as long as dogs are a clean black. I don't care much for blue-eyed dogs, and definitely prefer ones that will be a challenge to me.

Everyone involved in trialling undoubtedly has good and barren periods when things don't always go to plan. When I reach such a period it spurs me on to work harder, and if I like the dogs I am more motivated to work on any problems they might have and put them right. In 1997 the old Roy was having a tremendous season coming reserve at the International at Thurles, but by the summer of 1998 he wasn't running so well. I worked really hard with him straight after the International over the winter months and he finally won the International Supreme Champion title in 1999 at Aberystwyth. Of all the dogs I have had he was the best. Bob also won the International the following year at Armathwaite.

Luck also plays a small part at trials. I have seen bad sheep at trials and had good runs; I have also been to trials with good sheep and had bad runs. On balance I would say I am both lucky and unlucky. In trialling you have to accept that things do go wrong and as long as you have faith in your dogs the problems can be put right. I have a lot of faith in my current dogs, Mac and Roy. Both peaked too soon at the Nationals this year at Builth Wells, but that's how things are. I don't get disappointed and the older I get the more relaxed I become. Unfortunately so does everyone else!

(Information courtesy Medwen Lloyd Jones and Aled Owen.)

Guiding Principle

Pressure can be your best friend, and it can also be your worst enemy.

---

the sheep right up to the pen mouth without stopping and at a steady pace. Any sharp movements will apply unnecessary pressure on the sheep and might spook them. If you find that the sheep stand in the mouth of the pen and test the dog or are not in quite the right position, leave the dog in one position and apply the pressure on, pressure off technique. By moving backwards you might create a space for the sheep to move into; alternatively by moving on to the sheep you might help to push them into the pen, as a move towards the dog would almost always be out of the question.

The transition for both handler and young dog from working at home to competing in sheepdog trials needs to be carefully executed. Many handlers introduce their dog to the trials scene by taking them to trials and familiarizing them with the various aspects and elements involved, such as long journeys, travelling with other dogs, being chained up, taking off spent sheep after runs, and so on. If you can give your dog experience of working on different breeds of sheep, this too will pay dividends. The more trials you take your dog to, the more accustomed it will become, and the more at ease you will be. For handlers new to trialling, getting to know the other competitors should also be high on your agenda, as this will ease the pressure on you when you start to run your dog. By the time your dog is ready to compete in its first trial it should be equally at home on the trial field as your farm.

CHAPTER 13

SHEEPDOG TRIALS

Sheepdog trials, for me, are about making things happen, not about hoping that things will go my way. Also it is not taking part that matters, but winning. If there are six prizes to be had, only the first is good enough, as no one ever remembers the runner-up. I also admire and have the greatest respect for the handlers that have dogged determination, who rise to the challenge and who are in pursuit of perfection. What makes these handlers stand out from the rest is that they never accept defeat, they are meticulous in practising their art, and they are never satisfied. I admire a handler who recognizes the efforts of others and who, even in adversity, offers a hand to the successor in recognition of their success. What I admire

Walking to the post – time to be confident and decisive.

above all, however, is the handler who willingly imparts his knowledge and the secrets of his success so that others may benefit, without fear that the student may one day be better than the teacher. Only by helping others improve can handlers make it possible to raise the bar themselves.

From a judge's perspective, the handler who makes an effort to achieve perfection will always score higher than the handler who holds the dog back and just hopes that things will go right. Relying on hope simply makes you complacent, whereas attempting to achieve perfection makes you sharper. There is an old adage 'practice makes perfect': however, this is not always the case. If it were just a matter of practice, the level of competition at trials would be much higher. Practice does, however, make permanent, in that if what you are practising is wrong or flawed in some way, what you will achieve will also be flawed. You have to practise the right things, concentrate and remain focused on every training element.

In any given sport, success depends on 90 per cent training and 10 per cent luck. There are many handlers who appear lucky, such as Aled Owen. However, can luck alone account for three International Supreme titles and two World titles?

A handler who takes control of the situation is often the one whose dog is the most fluent, on the move and gets on with the job in a practical way. Remember that a judge has to sit in his car or trailer for up to ten hours, and only when a handler or dog really catches his eye will he sit up and take notice.

In short, be forthright and confident in your handling. And if you declare that you don't have confidence in your dog before you have even started, then this will affect not only how the dog runs for you, but also how you are perceived by the judge and other handlers. In such cases deal with those problems before you start trialling.

THE UNWRITTEN RULES OF TRIALLING

As with any sport, it is absolutely crucial that handlers familiarize themselves with the rules and etiquette that govern the sport. It is always easy to obtain the rules, as usually they are written down, but the only way you can familiarize yourself with the unwritten rules is by talking to people and observing the behaviour of runners. Even when rules are carved out in stone they are open to interpretation, and it is always a good idea to clarify certain points with the course director prior to running. Some might also think it a good idea to clarify aspects with other runners, however, as stated previously, their interpretation may be different to everyone else.

Furthermore, there is always an element of gamesmanship to contend with. I recall a Welsh friend of mine sitting by the entrance to the course at Clynnog, North Wales. As I had arrived only minutes before having to run, I asked him whether the line for the cross-drive was in front of the fetch gates or behind. He was renowned for having a dry sense of humour, and instantly looked me straight in the eye and replied 'Behind the fetch gates'. 'Are you sure?' I questioned, as the line looked in front to me. 'Of course,' he replied, and suggested I check with the course director. There wasn't enough time for that, however, as the previous runner had retired and it was my turn.

As I walked to the post with Skerry, I looked towards the fetch gates trying to decide whether he was joking or whether he might be telling the truth. I decided to judge the line on merit once the sheep had turned at the first drive gates. No sooner had they done so and were heading for the cross-drive than I knew straightaway that he had been joking. Thereon I successfully negotiated the final hurdles, and following a clean pen I walked towards him. Before I could speak he offered his hand to me and congratulated me on what turned out to be a winning run.

Dog perfectly placed to flank either side aided by handler making good use of a giant step ladder.

He taught me a valuable lesson that day: never be afraid to ask for advice, but also never be afraid to trust your own gut instincts. There was no malicious intent in his misguided advice, just a little devilment, and without characters like him, sheepdog trials would be very boring indeed.

A number of unwritten rules also exists among triallists; these vary according to geographical locations:

- I have observed, in North Wales particularly, that if a handler is having a poor run or misses an obstacle, especially in the Open class, he/she will signal to the judge and retire. I have nothing but the utmost respect for handlers that recognize that they are unlikely to do well, and are gracious enough to offer the opportunity to others that they may do well.

- The welfare of sheep at trials is absolutely paramount. Landowners and countrymen and women have for some years felt that there is a strong 'anti' brigade with respect to country pursuits and country life. The television programme 'One Man and His Dog' has publicized the working collie and given it celebrity status. Through careful editing the unsavoury elements of sheep work have sometimes ended up on the cutting room floor, and the general public has been led to believe that both the sheep and dogs always behave impeccably. It is the handler's responsibility, as well as that of the judge and course director, to ensure that stress on sheep is minimized.

- An aggressive attitude towards a dog is also frowned upon, including excessive shouting.
- It is expected that handlers will not walk their dogs to the post on the lead.
- Criticizing any judge publicly is also unacceptable. The judge is the only person on a trial field that looks at every aspect of every run and is best placed to make critical decisions. Bystanders often remark on something a judge did or a score given to a competitor, but can they really claim to have watched every run in detail?
- Whistles should not be used to control dogs whilst other competitors are running.
- Biosecurity – since the foot and mouth outbreaks in 2000 it has become of primary concern that dog, vehicles and handlers' clothes remain free of contaminants.
- Some judges will dock points for handlers who place their hands in their pockets, or even for leaning on the post.
- At some trials there is no post to stand by, and handlers stand either by the pen or in the pen mouth. It is crucial to find out what the rules are from the course director, prior to running. I have known handlers have a tremendous run only to find out afterwards that they have been docked points or even disqualified for standing in the wrong place.

QUALITY TIME FOR HANDLERS

Handlers also need time to prepare themselves. Many are up at the crack of dawn in order to get the jobs on the farm done, before travelling to trials. I recall enjoying driving and losing myself in my thoughts as I drove to trials in Derbyshire Peak District and Snowdonia National Park. The journey acted as a destressor. However, since the instigation of speed cameras, driving has become a chore and greater concentration is needed to maintain what often seem to be unnatural speeds on roads. If you have been flashed by a speed camera your mindset may be that of anger, not just for the rest of the day, but the whole week.

Prior to running a dog at a trial it is important that you take time out to relax, to blow away the cobwebs, and to get something to eat or even catch up on sleep. Minimizing verbal contact with your dog/s will ensure that you do not become more stressed, and are relaxed prior to running. As mentioned earlier, if you are not familiar with the idiosyncrasies of a particular region, then ask the course director about what is expected in terms of line of cross-drive, when to move to the pen, and so on. You could always ask another competitor, but gamesmanship and tomfoolery may dictate their answer. I have known many top handlers who after a long journey have run their dogs soon after arrival and ended up running the course in the wrong direction, taking the sheep to the cross-drive gates before the first drive. I have also known handlers to attempt a shed before penning, based on information received from 'friendly competitors', when the shed element was not required. It is so easily done.

PREPARING FOR YOUR RUN

Over the years there has been much debate as to the whether handlers ought to walk their dog to the post on a lead. The assumption that most people would make in such circumstances is that the dog cannot be trusted to walk to the post, thereby begging the question: can it be trusted on the trial field? Some judges have been known to, controversially, dock points for doing this. My view is; if there is a risk that any aspect of your handling might lead to close scrutiny or come under question, then alter your ways. Most judging is subjective and you will rarely if ever change a judge's view, but you can change what you do.

If you do go to the post with your dog on the lead there is a good chance that your dog is *not* ready and in the correct position for the start of the outrun when you get there. Sheep don't always wait conveniently for you whilst you remove the lead and put it away. The short walk from the judge's car or trailer is one of the most crucial periods of time that any handler ever has. During this time you need to:

- Ensure your dog cannot see the sheep from the previous run being taken off.
- Get yourself composed and calm by taking deep breaths.
- Locate the sheep, and the direction they are moving in.
- Identify whether you need to change the direction of the outrun.
- Manoeuvre the dog to the side in which it will outrun.
- Stand still and ask your dog to look for the sheep.
- Ensure that your dog is close to you or the post, but far enough away so that you are not interfering with its vision or putting undue pressure on it.
- Walk to the post in a confident manner.
- Finally, before sending the dog on its outrun, ensure that its head is turned away from you and in the direction you want it to run.
- Give a clear, concise command to avoid confusion.

If, and only if, you can ensure that you go through the above ritual every time you walk to the post, will your dog stand a good chance of doing well.

Identifying the Risk Factors

Many handlers make the mistake of building up certain trials, for example the Nationals, thereby placing greater pressure on themselves to perform. No matter what the trial is, it is the assessment of what risks you need to take that will make the difference at the end of the day. The Nationals and Internationals, above all other trials, are different in that detailed scores are provided for the different elements so handlers can watch and compare runs, and gauge how the judges are awarding or taking off the marks. This information can provide you with the basis of what risks you need to take, for example whether to give extra blow-out whistles, or wait for your dog to make a mistake before acting.

Some handlers are, of course, very cautious about risk taking, whilst others are braver. Fortune does not always favour the brave, however.

Knowing your dog is part of the assessment you need to consider. Making a list of their strengths and weaknesses will enable you to calculate what actions you might want or need to take, given the type of trial you are competing in. Comparing these with the scoring at trials will give you enough courage to plan how to run your dog, and where to take the risks and where to play safe.

Whether you choose to take risks or not, I am fatalistic enough to believe that ultimately if it is written, you will win. At every trial someone invariably wins the day, and sometimes it appears beyond reason why the sheep reacted in the way they did, and why they accepted certain dogs more happily than others. It is these unknown factors that make trialling so exciting.

Concentration

How much do I need to concentrate? This might

seem an obvious question, but anyone who has ever run dogs will tell you that the unexpected always happens. There are many factors that make trialling exciting. The weather can be as crucial to how the sheep behave as the lie of the land. Coping with nerves is another pitfall; for instance there is nothing worse than the sound of laughter behind you when you are running a dog, or people talking.

Familiarizing yourself with the potential pitfalls can be a huge advantage – but although you can walk the course and establish where the line of the cross-drive is compared to the fetch gates, nevertheless this information can become the very cause of your downfall. The secret is to bear everything in mind, but to be open and flexible. I have analysed the lie of the ground many times, or the angle of the obstacles, religiously measured the distance from the fetch gates to the line of the cross-drive, and still missed an obstacle. The reason for this is quite simple: the calculations were not carried out from the post, therefore accuracy is not guaranteed.

Watch how the sheep behave for other people, where they place their dogs, where the dog is on approaching the gates, whether the dog is lying down or standing, what angle it is at to turn the sheep correctly. Learning to 'read' the leading ewe is also crucial.

One of the most important attributes of a good handler is peripheral vision. Whether you are training a dog or competing in a trial, your awareness of obstacles, where the sheep are, and external factors such as dead spots, is of the utmost importance. Many times I have seen dogs running very well and then all of a sudden they miss an obstacle. Don't ever assume that the sheep are through the gate: just make sure that they are. Often gates placed at an angle can distort what you actually see, thereby decreasing the observable distance between two gates.

Trialling is like a game of snooker: you don't simply pot the balls, you need to plan ahead as to where to place the white ball following each successful shot in order to pot the next. Top handlers don't just aim to put the sheep through the first drive obstacle: rather, they plan meticulously where the dog should be on approaching obstacles in order to achieve a tight turn. As soon as the sheep have negotiated the hurdle and settle, handlers then assess the line and distance to the next hurdle, often making ongoing assessments of the accuracy, in trying to successfully negotiate the cross-drive gate. Once again, on approaching the cross-drive gate they will know exactly where they want the dog, in order to achieve a good turn, and thereafter a straight line to the centre of the shedding ring or pen.

Gates that are sometimes placed on an incline can be deceptive particularly if, as in Derbyshire, they are of a 'pull through' nature, so the sheep may look as if they are comfortably behind the line of the gates, but actually the ground drops and brings them forwards with each step.

Some dogs' hearing appears to be a lot more acute than others, yet some of these dogs are noticeably hindered in some circumstances, whereas other dogs are not. I have competed at the Open Sheepdog Trial at Dolgellau, at Fronalchen Fields in North Wales, since the early 1990s. The trial field is flanked by ancient woodland on one side, and a steep bank on the other, and about a hundred metres or so behind the handler's post there is a river running through it. Each year I compete there and am amazed at how some dogs obviously hear the commands with absolutely no trouble at all, whilst others appear not to be able to hear any of them, whether whistle or voice. It is almost as if the sound is carried away and lost in the woodland.

Similarly at Longshaw Sheepdog Trials, in Derbyshire, the dogs have to negotiate a bank on the first drive element. I have observed many

A league of gentlemen – the England Team 2006.

dogs becoming confused and looking back at the handlers as though they had not heard the command properly. Once again it is highly likely that the commands went over the top of the bank. However, in some cases dogs became confused even before they had gone down the bank into the hollow.

In both the above scenarios I have observed handlers trying new ways of communicating with their dogs, sometimes in the vain hope that they would connect with the dog in time to negotiate the obstacle. The most common approach was to change from whistle to verbal commands; some lowered themselves to ground level, so that the sound might carry more easily, whilst others cupped their hands together to direct the sound better. I also observed handlers turning to one side and giving both verbal and whistle commands, as well as using a lower pitch on the whistle rather than a higher one.

Weather also plays a part in making life difficult at such trials, particularly when it is windy. Although a whistle sound cuts through the atmosphere far more readily than verbal commands, natural obstacles such as trees, nevertheless offer the greatest challenge, when they join forces with adverse weather conditions. There is nothing worse than blowing a whistle against a strong headwind or when it is raining.

I recall competing at the English National Sheepdog Trials in 2006, at Kirby Lonsdale, where many dogs missed the first drive obstacle as the noise from the nearby trade-stand flags was making it difficult for the dogs to hear. I ran Spot first and struggled to make myself heard, so when I ran Skerry I was ready to use verbal commands if the whistles failed. This is exactly what happened, and thanks to my swapping to verbal commands, Skerry negotiated the first drive successfully, despite some panic on my part, and went on to complete the course, finishing sixth.

Again in 2006, this time at the International held at Kelso, in the Scottish Borders, external factors played a big part, though on this occasion explanations were not quite so obvious or clear. The course was flat, with hedges to the side and rear, and due to the size of the course, dogs running to the hedges ran out too wide. The qualifying rounds were largely uneventful, although I did lose Skerry on her outrun, having given her an extra cautionary whistle to go out. Once she took the extra whistle, she cast out wide and despite further attempts to call her in again, she seemed to be deaf to my calls. The same was true for one or two dogs that circled their sheep on the cross-drive gates to the left of the handler. These dogs were seasoned dogs with experience and longevity in their favour, yet they behaved like nursery dogs.

The running in some cases on the final day was embarrassing for some of the handlers. Many of the dogs appeared not only to ignore commands from their handlers, but to push the sheep away from them, towards the left-hand hedge, almost as though they believed that their handler was on that side. I heard many criticize the dogs for not being able to complete a fetch to the handler, and describe the International as one of the worst. Yet it was beyond coincidence that so many dogs behaved out of character, at the same time, and it was too easy for spectators and bystanders to criticize the performance of dogs and handlers that day; however, the fact that so many top handlers were found wanting certainly gave credence to the theory of 'dead or deaf spots'. Trialling is a great leveller, and on that day I believe nature played a far more significant part than many were willing to accept. In all cases take nothing for granted, and you won't be disappointed.

NURSERY TRIALS

The purpose of nursery trials is to school or educate young dogs. You can give them experience in a variety of settings, away from the comforts of home, but with the same watchful and critical eye that you have whilst training at home. Success at nursery trials should not be defined in terms of which dogs are placed in the top six; rather you should consider your dog to be successful if it runs to its potential, or just as it does at home. Some societies have progressive trials so that the earlier trials are easier, often with shorter outruns and no shed elements. As the season progresses, trials often become more and more challenging, not only in terms of the elements one has to complete, but also the size of the course.

The sheep at nursery trials are often hoggs, which at the start of the season are not used to being worked in small numbers, so they can be quite difficult to manage. Therefore it is not unusual that the dogs that are successful are either very careful workers that don't upset sheep, or those that have a lot of experience of farm work and are therefore not fazed by flighty sheep. Dogs with a lot of eye also tend to do well with flighty sheep.

If you have the sort of dog that needs time and a lot of work to fulfil its potential, you will have to be content with achieving success in small portions. These dogs are often slow to mature and need time and patience, but in the end make far better all round dogs, which are not only able to move large flocks, but also develop the sensitivity to work with flightier hill breeds.

Regardless of how good a young dog is at Nursery level, all dogs need time to grow, mature and develop confidence in their own ability and in their handler. Time is significant,

Flock of Hebrideans – ideal for training dogs. They can be flighty, but are just as likely to turn on a dog.

Mule ewes – they can be flighty, but are also stubborn and imposing to a young dog.

and probably the most crucial of elements to future success. I have seen many dogs pushed into Nursery trials between twelve and fifteen months, but early success at trials usually only serves to put value on them if they are to be sold on. The Lewis Hamiltons (World youngest Formula One racing driver champion) of the dog world are few and far between, and the numbers that go on to achieve success in Open trials are significantly low when compared to the numbers that compete. Remember, dogs need to learn to read sheep, as do handlers: hoggs behave totally differently to older ewes, and hill sheep are different to heavier lowland types, and only through experience of these various types can the dog become an all round performer.

Keep a realistic eye on your dog, and if you like what you have, then you will always end up with a dog that performs well at Open level. In Nursery trials keep an open mind, lower your threshold of expectation, and you will not be disappointed. Remember, young dogs will make mistakes, but you cannot afford to, if you want to achieve success as a triallist. Use each trial as a training opportunity, and learn from your mistakes.

There is no reason why at a Nursery trial you cannot tell the judge that you would like to have a training run, and ask them not to score you. At least this way you are not under pressure, and can concentrate on making sure that your dog does things correctly. Some judges will appreciate this, as it gives them a break from concentration.

I am a keen advocate of Cradle trials,

although these days they are very scarce, as are the Class Threes that were synonymous in North Wales. However, some regions still have Local classes or Young Handler classes, which serve the same purpose. These are not only useful for schooling young dogs, but are also immensely helpful to novice or young handlers who are new to trialling. Although they vary between regions, the principle is initially to have just outrun, lift and first drive elements in the early season, and then gradually build in the cross-drive, shed and so on. I would advocate Nursery trials building in Cradle trials, as this way the running would not take as long as it does, due to the course being shorter, as well as the length of time. Most importantly, young dogs would not be pushed so hard and would

be given the time to mature. It is also common practice for many dog disciplines to limit the age at which dogs can compete in order to safe-guard their health and development.

Health and fitness are uppermost in the minds of all handlers, because if a dog becomes ill or injured it is the equivalent to losing one's 'right arm man'. For many farmers missing a few trials is one thing, but losing the services of a good dog can affect their livelihood. Neverthe-less, just as farming has evolved over the centuries, so has the means of keeping dogs fit and healthy and in tip-top condition for work. And for those in search of information about any of these matters, being able to 'Google' the world wide web means having the answers to any question at the tips of their fingers.

Jacobs require a calm but strong dog; they can invite a grip, and provide a true test for dogs of any age.

CHAPTER 14

HEALTH AND FITNESS

PREVENTION IS BETTER THAN CURE

I have spent the past five years watching my son play basketball, and have seen the gruelling regime of fitness he has had to follow, combined with the injuries he has suffered – and this has made me reflect that as shepherds and triallists we do not pay nearly enough attention to our dog's fitness or to preventing them from getting injured. In any discipline or walk of life, prevention is better than cure, and people should take great heed of this age-old sentiment.

WARMING UP AND COOLING DOWN

The warm-up is a preparation phase before exercise, and the purpose of this is to increase the body temperature by approximately 1 to 2°F, thereby protecting dogs against injury. Horses are walked and trotted for several minutes on a lunge line or under saddle, or occasionally on a treadmill or horse walker if such equipment is available. Can you imagine the dire consequences of a show jumper attempting to jump big fences from cold after coming straight out of his box? It would not happen.

For racing greyhounds, five to ten minutes of brisk walking or jogging prior to racing is recommended. A specific warm-up is believed to improve skill and coordination. Sports that require accuracy, timing and precise movements tend to benefit from some type of specific preliminary practice.

Preparing your collie for work is one of the most crucial elements of sheep work I know of, apart from training. Good preparation is a must for anyone who competes or works their dog in any discipline, and it needs careful management not only prior to work, but also after. Most, if not all competitors let their dogs out of their car several minutes prior to running them in sheepdog trials, but how many of these do so to warm up or limber up their dogs, rather than just giving them the opportunity to relieve themselves? If a dog jumps straight out of the car or kennel and starts working, it will tire a lot sooner than if it has had time to warm up. Of course there are bound to be exceptions to the rule, and also the dog's age and fitness have a great bearing on this.

The idea of warming up your dogs might bring a smile to the face of some of you, but in reality your dog is every bit an athlete as any professional sportsman or woman. In every sport, professional athletes warm up between thirty minutes to an hour prior to competing. Each group of muscles in turn is warmed up and stretched to avoid injury. Warming up does not simply offer you the opportunity for peak performance and endurance; rather it pre-empts injury and strain. Unfortunately, dogs

Poetry in a visual form.

cannot tell us when they are in pain, often working through the pain barrier until they can stand it no more.

I recall my own Lara who, just prior to the English National in 2001, suffered a partial dislocation of her shoulder. Following this serious injury she was x-rayed thoroughly, and I was quite shocked to be informed that at some point in her life she had sustained a broken bone in her toes, which had subsequently healed. I had no knowledge of this. Similarly I have spoken to footballers who have had x-rays and surgery in the later years of their career, and been told that there was evidence of previous fractures, which they knew nothing about.

New materials and fibres, such as compression shorts and vests, are now used by sportsmen to ensure that the risk of injury is minimized.

It is great that scientists have provided us with the means to improve performance beyond a whole new level, which once would have been unimaginable, however, even now when we are armed with such information I notice young sportsmen and their coaches not putting enough emphasis on warming up and cooling down. The same I am sure will apply to the dog world. In life there are sceptics and believers just as there are winners and losers. Some resent change whilst others relish and embrace

---

Guiding Principle

Knowledge is the greatest of all gifts, but the ability to act on knowledge is far greater.

---

it. The question to ask yourself is, 'What harm can it do'?

Sheep work, above all other disciplines, is one of the most gruelling for a Border Collie, in terms of the time spent working, the physical demands and stamina. A small investment of time will ensure that warm-ups and cool-downs lessen the risk of injury. A cost in time is always better than a financial burden. Warm-ups and cool-downs also ensure your dog is always at his/her peak before competing, therefore better able to achieve his/her potential.

There is also nothing worse than making a long journey on a cold winter's day, then asking the dog to jump straight out of the car and expecting him to perform to the best of his ability. Most of us can't function in the mornings until we have had a coffee, yet we expect our dogs to gear themselves up for work in an instance. Their minds may well be willing, but their bodies will need time to adapt, especially if they are quite old or past their youthful best.

About thirty or forty minutes prior to running your dog, take them for a good walk or run.

Spot, affectionately known as 'my boy'. He always gives 100 per cent even when only 50 per cent is required.

Skye, unmistakably a daughter of Aled Owen's Roy.

Some handlers are cautious about letting their dogs run too much in case they tire. However, when a dog runs he releases endorphins, and this will ensure that he then wants to run all the more. The procedures mentioned above are all the more important when dealing with an older dog, as the potential for harm or injury or below par performance is all the greater. There are many competitors in other dog disciplines who even go to the extent of stretching out their dogs' limbs prior to performing.

COOLING DOWN

Cooling down after exercise is just as important as warming up in order to facilitate speedy muscle recovery and the dispersal of lactic acid. This reduces the risk of muscle soreness. Diane Schuller (*see* References) in her article for *Dogs in Canada* entitled 'Ready, set warm-up', writes about a physiotherapist trained in animal physical therapy and rehabilitation, who recommends that the cool-down period should consist of a minimum of twenty minutes of walking after strenuous exercise. For many of us it would take longer to drive the dog to the vet!

LEAVING DOGS IN CARS

This is a subject that has been close to my heart for many years, ever since my dog Lara suffered from heatstroke. Having arrived at the sheepdog trial in Tackley, Oxfordshire, I exercised Lara as usual in extreme hot temperatures. As Lara was the only dog I had to run, it was less than an hour before my run. Following a short walk, I put Lara back into my car, into a purpose-built dog cage, which enabled me to leave the back, as well as all the windows open. Being a hot

Energy and the Working Dog

by Dr Angie Untisz DVM

In 2004 Dr Untisz's Kelpie, Dodge, developed a potentially life-threatening condition called 'exertional rhabdomyolysis', commonly called 'tying up'. An alarming set of symptoms developed, culminating in his collapsing while training. His body was breaking down muscle tissue in an attempt to generate the energy source it so desperately needed. Dr Untisz knew she would have to find a solution before her talented partner literally worked himself to death. With nutrition research in hand she delved further into the world of canine athletics. Using Sled dogs as a model for her research, she opened gateways to information resulting in Glyco-Gen, the product that gave Dodge the energy he needed to continue his competitive career.

Working dogs are truly premier canine athletes, and as such, one should pay close attention to meeting their energy needs. There are three sources of energy: fats, carbohydrates and proteins. Understanding how the working dog utilizes energy and how best to balance these energy stores can result in a more responsive partner that is less prone to physical injury.

Fats are the most energy dense of all the sources, providing 70–90 per cent of the energy needed for muscle contraction (primarily fuelling slow-twitch fibres). In the working dog, 50–65 per cent of total energy in a diet should come from fats. (This translates to 25–32.5 per cent fat on a dry matter basis.) When fed a high fat diet, the working dog will develop pathways that promote aerobic oxidation of free fatty acids (fat adaptation). In addition, adding an anti-oxidant such as Vitamin E and the amino acid l-carnitine can improve the muscle's use of fat. Aerobic oxidation of free fatty acids leads to less lactic acid build-up in the muscle, and better endurance capability.

Carbohydrates are stored in muscle as glycogen. Muscle uses glycogen during the initial moments of activity and for bursts of speed and power (primarily fuelling fast twitch fibres). Glycogen stores are relatively small and can be rapidly depleted, leading to muscle weakness and fatigue. However, diets high in carbohydrates can lead to reconditioning (poor endurance, obesity and muscle injury). For a working dog, carbohydrates should be limited to 10–15 per cent of the total energy in the diet. To

---

day I ensured she had plenty to drink. However, when I next let her out of the car she jumped down and fell to the ground. She had shown no signs of distress, but then I realized later that she had not been panting either, which would have served to cool her down.

As she lay there, a crowd gathered round me, one of whom was Ray Edwards. Ray rushed to his car and swiftly returned with a sachet of 'Lectade' in his hand. Tearing it open, he mixed a solution of it into a bowl of water, which I gave to Lara by hand, initially. Within half an hour Lara was back up on her feet, though I didn't consider running her. Forearmed with this knowledge I was never to take that chance again, and always ensured that there was Lectade in the car. Although Lara did suffer once again with a 'heat stroke', this time whilst working, I was prepared, and neither of us went through the same trauma as we had done at Tackley.

A year or so later I was to discover a similar solution to Lectade, but in powder form, and in

improve the working dog's use of carbohydrates, one should focus on replenishing glycogen stores and slowing glycogen depletion.

Replenishing glycogen stores is accomplished by providing a 'good' carbohydrate at an appropriate time. Muscle cells have GLUT4 pathways that are active during exercise and for up to thirty minutes after exercise. These pathways allow for the uptake of carbohydrate into the muscle without the release of insulin. Simple sugars (glucose, dextrose, fructose, corn syrup) cause an insulin release, which leads to subsequent hypoglycaemia (low blood sugar). Complex starches (bread, rice, grains) take too long to be digested and absorbed. Both cause fluid imbalances that can contribute to diarrhoea and dehydration. Maltodextrin is a small, complex carbohydrate and is ideal for this purpose. It is rapidly absorbed without an insulin release or fluid imbalance, and is readily utilized by the GLUT4 pathway. When a Maltodextrin supplement is given within thirty minutes of exercise, up to 85 per cent of pre-exercise glycogen levels are restored. Without this targeted approach, only 40 per cent of pre-exercise levels are restored.

Slowing the depletion of glycogen stores is accomplished in two ways. First, when enough fat is fed, slow twitch fibres will use free fatty acids as their energy source (fat adaptation), sparing glycogen for use by fast twitch fibres. Second, supplementation prior to activity with a 'good' carbohydrate such as Maltodextrin will give the working dog a little carbohydrate 'to burn' before starting on the glycogen stores. It is very important to avoid simple sugars and starches so as to avoid insulin spikes and fluid imbalances.

Proteins are the building blocks of muscle, and should not be a major source of energy. Animal source proteins – chicken, beef, lamb, egg – are preferred, and often offer increased digestibility with a good amino acid balance. Diets low in protein have been associated with increased injuries. A working dog diet should have a minimum 26 per cent protein. For hard-working dogs, diets containing 30–40 per cent proteins are even better. The goal is to spare the use of proteins as an energy source so these can be used to build muscle mass and repair muscle damage.

In summary, working dogs should be fed a diet high in fat to optimize energy availability, and high in proteins to protect against injury. Carbohydrates should be supplemented at appropriate times to improve their storage. Remember, feed for energy and you will have energetic dogs.

(Courtesy Dr Angie Untisz DVM Bend OR.)

---

a plastic container, which made it more practical to administer as necessary and without wastage. Soon I was giving the powder to all the dogs in their food, in particular before intensive physical exercise as well as after, and began to notice the benefit not just in stamina but also in their recovery from exercise. There were also noticeably fewer instances of muscle tying up and stiffness following rigorous work – although this may also have been due to cooling down.

More recently, following a chance discussion with a sheepdog triallist from America in 2008 who had come across Dr Angie Untisz, who like me, had similar experience of her dog suffering muscle tie-up. She conducted research in order to find a solution to the problem, and her story is detailed in the panel.

TREADMILLS

Many people are now investing in treadmills for

The future belongs to the young – Skye with Tess, bred back to Bobby Dalziel's Jim.

mineral and animal worlds, homoeopathic remedies have proved to be safe when used with conventional medicines.

People have turned increasingly to homoeopathy, both for human ailments and for the treatment of animals. Historically the world of medicine and homoeopathy remained very much apart; nowadays, however, it is more accepted for the two to complement each other, and indeed homoeopathic remedies are now commonplace and can be found on supermarket shelves. They work by gently boosting the natural energy of the body, and are safe, without risk of addiction or toxicity. Homoeopathic remedies have been used by people to treat sore throats and acute fevers, as well as chronic

larly other bitches, suffered a loss of appetite, and her performance at sheepdog trials, during this period, became noticeably poor. My friend had come across this type of problem before and recommended a homoeopathic practitioner, who recommended using pulsatilla and sepia during Lara's pre-oestrus period. Almost instantly I observed an improvement in Lara's mood and appetite, and her levels of concentration, whilst working, noticeably improved. The added bonus was that I did not have to pay extortionate consultation fees to vets, as the homoeopaths were more than happy not only to discuss but also to research on my behalf possible remedies, which cost only a few pounds. Combined with the fact that there were no worrying side effects, this alternative option began to look very appealing.

Being involved in any sport inevitably involves injury, and it wasn't long before I began thinking about using homoeopathic remedies to treat injuries. I was no longer the sceptic I once was, having experienced some success, and enquired about possible treatments to enhance recovery from injury. Remedies such as ruta grav and rhus tox, as well as arnica, the best known of the three, became regular items in my dog first aid box, which always travels with me.

Increasingly I began to share my experience with other dog owners, and suddenly everyone had similar experiences to share about natural remedies. The following are alternative or natural remedies that I have used to good effect with my own dogs, following advice from practitioners, and the conditions they treat:

illnesses such as arthritis, eczema, asthma, mild depression and chronic fatigue syndrome, to mention a few.

My fascination with homoeopathy began in 1992 when I was introduced to it by a friend. Lara was a fairly biddable dog, but she would experience a personality change up to six or eight weeks before she came into season. She would become intolerant of other dogs, particu-

- Denes garlic tablets: arthritis, fleas
- Denes greenleaf: arthritis
- Silicea or silica: thorns, splinters
- Salt and apple cider vinegar: thorns, splinters
- Colloidal silver: cuts and grazes
- Rhus tox: physical injury, knocks, sprains
- Ruta grav: physical injury, knocks, sprains

- Arnica: physical injury, knocks, sprains, bruising
- Pulsatilla: pre-oestrus/hormonal problems
- Sepia: pre-oestrus/hormonal problems

Three of the above-mentioned remedies have a vast number of different uses associated with them, namely garlic, colloidal silver and apple cider vinegar. It is recommended that you research these, as they have implications for other livestock, too.

In 2004 Spot suddenly took to refusing to go around handlers who were letting sheep out at trials. There was no way of knowing what might have caused the problem, and it did cross my mind whether something or someone might have inadvertently caused him to become frightened or anxious about running past them. Spot would happily run out but as soon as he came to the first handler letting the sheep out he would cut in front and refuse any stop commands, proceeding to bring the sheep towards me at a rate of knots. He even began to do the same thing on home territory, with people he knew. I turned to a homoeopath by the name of Frances Gavin. After a discussion with her over the telephone she recommended a remedy called Sanper, one of her own products. Spot was given a single tablet each day for nearly two months, in addition to following a programme of socialization, which involved introducing him to new experiences; going into the village, travelling on the bus, visiting people. Incidentally these were new experiences for me, too! After five or six weeks he began to turn the corner, until finally after two months the problem was completely resolved. Spot was never to repeat this type of behaviour again.

Injuries

Frances Gavin became the first person I would contact when I had a query as to the treatment of behaviour, injuries or breeding-related problems. What I particularly liked about Frances was that she combined different remedies within a single tablet – for example her 'A-Combo', which I use for treating injuries, combines ruta grav, rhus tox and arnica, thereby making the administration of tablets to dogs a lot simpler.

Dogs, and particularly young dogs, have a tremendous capability for healing after serious injury, and the stories of dogs recovering from horrendous injury are abundant on the trials circuit. This is hardly surprising when you look at how single-minded the Border Collie is in its pursuit of work with sheep. Dogs are eternal optimists, unlike humans, and they do not worry about the past or the future, but live in the here and now.

My own dogs are line bred to my own Fly, and have always shown tremendous courage in the event of injury – there is never any wallowing in self pity or feeling sorry for themselves. Twelve months ago Fly ripped her hind foot down to the bone, an injury that needed stitching, but the very next day she was first in the car wanting to come to the farm – she simply ran on three legs, putting down the injured one every now and again to balance herself. My Spot suffered severe ligament damage two weeks before the 2007 English National in the North Yorkshire Moors, yet he was still happy go for walks and gently follow the sheep out on the moors.

Both Spot and Fly were treated using homoeopathic remedies. I was told Spot would never work again without limping, yet he has worked better than ever since the injury and without needing surgery. Often it is the handler who feels the pain most, born out of guilt for the dog getting injured, and humanizing the situation. It can be incredibly difficult to separate the needs of the dog from the needs of the handler. Time and patience are great healers, coupled with a positive mindset.

About Frances Gavin

Frances Gavin has been a dog behaviourist since the 1980s, and set up Canine Natural Cures over twenty years ago when she discovered how much dogs and owners could be helped when homoeopathy and training are combined. Having developed a particular interest in alternative approaches to health and healing, Frances gained diplomas in homoeopathy and nutrition as well as being a Reiki Master.

Over the past seven years Frances has proved an invaluable source of information, and some of her recommendations to me are detailed below. It should, however, be borne in mind that if you have any serious doubts about the health of your dogs then you should contact a veterinarian first.

Pregnancy

Raspberry leaf is well recognized as the traditional birthing herb – you can give it throughout pregnancy to help make whelping trouble free. Also give caulophyllum once daily for the last four weeks of pregnancy to aid delivery. During labour you can give pulsatilla every half hour, or use rescue remedy and after whelping give one dose of sepia to help the uterus return to normal. Extra vitamin C during pregnancy helps develop strong, well-boned pups, and a vitamin B complex will help prevent birth defects. Phantom pregnancy will be helped by sepia or pulsatilla. Frances provides a homoeopathic whelping pack especially to help bitches whelping for the first time or which have had difficulty whelping in the past.

Stud Dogs

Vitamin E is vital for a stud dog, and he needs twice as much as usual for a couple of weeks before a service. Give him extra eggs, too, as these contain selenium. For dogs whose performance is less than enthusiastic, try ginseng or damiana. Royal jelly is said to improve sperm production!

First Aid Kit

- Colloidal silver as an all-purpose disinfectant for injuries such as cuts; it is also excellent for upset stomachs.
- Bach Flower's rescue remedy – use a few drops on the tongue in the event of shock and trauma, or give aconite.
- Apis mel for bee or wasp stings.
- Arnica is used for bruises, sprains and torn muscles, in post operative treatment, or for any injury. You can safely give a dose every hour or so while the dog seems to be in pain or limping; the improvement should be apparent after a few hours.
- Ruta and rhus tox are also recommended for sprains and strains.
- Ledum is for puncture wounds, especially if a bite is involved.

Nervous Behaviour

You can try one of the following: aconite, argent. nit, gelsemium, nux vomica, phosphorus or pulsatilla:

- Pulsatilla: for the dog that follows you everywhere.
- Phosphorus: for dogs frightened by loud noises.
- Gelsemium: for the dog shaking with fear.
- Nux vomica: for the dog that may snap in fear.
- Aconite: for a frightened dog that has had a shock.
- Argent. Nit: for the dog frightened of going to the vet.

All the above remedies are available at your local health food store in 30c potency. Try a remedy, one tablet three times a day, for up to seven days. If there is no change in your dog, try a different remedy.

(Information courtesy of Frances Gavin.)

EPILOGUE

There is something very comforting about an old pair of slippers, a worn pair of boots or your favourite armchair. The mind is just the same. We get older and set in our own ways, of doing things in a particular way and sticking with tried and tested formulas. The world changes every second, and whilst the young embrace change and crave knowledge, the not-so-young are faced with a choice: that of moving with the times, or risking being left behind. Of course there are many who will say that youth is wasted on the young, and there have been times when I, too, thought the same, probably out of envy.

Most people my age (forty-six years old) grew up believing that no one would ever beat the 4-minute mile, after Roger Bannister did so in 1954 – but fifty-five years later it is now a standard for all professional athletes, and it has been bettered by a further 17 seconds since then. Only today I asked a well known sheepdog triallist competitor whether he had seen the English National venue at the Filleigh estate, South Molton, in Devon, and was somewhat taken aback by the response: 'No, I haven't been there, but I've had a look at it on Google Earth.'

Winners by nature will want to be the best, the fastest, climb the highest mountain, simply because it is there. No matter what obstacle is placed in their way, all they think about is overcoming it. They are prepared to go the extra mile to gain advantage, and some also become obsessed. Modern man might be far removed from the Stone Age hunter gatherer, but the same instincts that drove man then, still prevail today, just as our dogs mirror the behaviour exhibited by wolves. It's in the blood, so to speak. I am not blessed with a family history of farmers or triallists, nor do I own my own hill farm, yet each morning I wake up feeling blessed that at least in my mind lies a world that has all this and much more. Is this enough? It has to be.

Progress is inevitable in every walk of life, and there is no doubt in my mind that training sheepdogs and competing in sheepdog trials will without doubt undergo transitions and change. I have been very lucky to have been able to watch some great handlers working with equally great dogs, and to be able to ask their advice on the finer points of training Border Collies. It is a sad, but nevertheless true fact that each year we say goodbye to a generation of dog men whose wealth of knowledge is perhaps as precious as life itself. As with all sports, to ensure continuity the old and the wise, the great and the good owe it to themselves to pass on their wisdom to the young, about trialling and training sheepdogs for farm work. Only then will the sport continue to flourish, and in doing so keep farming and country life in the forefront. James Hogg, otherwise known as the 'Ettrick Shepherd', wrote in the eighteenth century: 'Without the Shepherd's dog, the whole of the open mountainous land in Scotland would not be worth a sixpence.' The value of Border Collies to farmers, and in turn the economy and environment, is immeasurable, and this book is as much a tribute to this wonderful breed of dog as the men who work alongside them.

As a young man of twenty-two I once heard the lead singer of a reggae band, Delbert 'Ngoni'

Tyson of Misty in Roots, start the concert with the following quote: 'Without the knowledge of your history you cannot determine your destiny.' Although I was never to forget this quote, the meaning of it was not so apparent to me until I was in my thirties. I hold each one of my eighteen years in trialling as wholeheartedly precious, and shall be eternally grateful to those ladies and gentlemen, with whom I share my weekends at sheepdog trials, for so warm heartedly allowing me to share the countryside and their hobby.

I truly hope that this book will go some way to immortalize the thoughts, memories and advice of those handlers who have been so gracious as to share their wisdom with me, and who have helped me find both success and peace of mind. I have tried to give sheepdog training a makeover by introducing new concepts and redefining old ones, and bringing them into the twenty-first century whilst retaining its time-honoured and traditional aims and objectives. For those who have taken the time and trouble of reading this book I hope it will not just be useful, but will bring you success on the trial field. Above all, whichever path you choose with your dog or dogs, I dearly hope that you will experience the same pleasure I experience each and every day when my dogs run out on to the Caudal Hills in search of their sheep.

REFERENCES

Outcomes of breeding
http://www.optigen.com/opt9_test_cea_ch.ht
ml, 18 September 2009

Centralised Progressive Retinal Atrophy (PRA)
http://www.furrycritter.com/health/dogs/pdf/
Progressive_retinal_atrophy.pdf, 18 September 2009

Trapped Neutrophil Syndrome (TNS)
http://www.babs.unsw.edu.au/canine_genetics_facility_tns.php, 10 September 2009

The Volhard Puppy Aptitude Test
http://www.volhard.com/pages/resources.php,
18 March 2009

Orwell, G. J., Dutton/Signet April 1996 50th edition intro. From *Animal Farm* by George Orwell (Copyright George Orwell, 1945) by permission of Bill Hamilton as the Literary Executor of the Late Sonia Brownell Orwell and Secker & Warburg Ltd.

Gregory, *N. Animal Welfare and Meat Science, CAB International (1998).*
http://knol.google.com/k/clive-dalton/animal-behaviour-and-welfare-basic
17 April 2009

Millan, C. *Cesar's Way*, Hodder Paperbacks, London (7 February 2008). Offset by arrangements with Harmony books, an imprint of Crown Publishing group, a division of Random House Inc., New York.

Millan, C. *Be the Pack Leader*, Hodder Paperbacks, London (July 2009). Offset by arrangements with Harmony books, an imprint of Crown Publishing group, a division of Random House Inc., New York.

Stavroff, D. *Let the Dog Decide – The Revolutionary 15-minute-a-day Program to Train Your Dog – Gently and Reliably* (p. 191), Marlowe & Co. (10 January 2007).

Wagner, K., Van, 2009 on Albert Bandura
http://psychology.about.com/od/profilesofmajorthinkers/p/bio_bandura.htm
03/11/2009.

Bandura, A. Prof. and Woods, R. G., 1989
http://scholar.lib.vt.edu/theses/available/etd-040999-201108/unrestricted/CHP2.PDF

Seaward, B.L., December 2005, *Managing Stress: Principles and Strategies for Health and Well-Being,* 5th edition, p. 108, Jones and Bartlett Publishers, Inc.

Main, S. – National and International Winners 1906–2006
http://www.mainbordercollies.com/Nat__Int_Winners_1906_-_2006.html

Stanley Coren PhD and Sarah Hodgson, *Understanding a Dog's Sense of Smell* (p. 103), John Wiley & Sons (15 June 2007)

Owens, P. *The Dog Whisperer: A Compassionate, Nonviolent Approach to Dog Training* (p. 105). By Paul Owens, Norma Eckroate; Adams Media Corporation; 2nd revised edition (1 March 2007).

Monty Roberts, http://www.montyroberts.com (3 August 2009).

Schuller – Dogs in Canada www.dogsincanada.com/ready-set-warm-up). October 2008.

Vyas, N., http://www.nijvyassheepdogs.com

Vyas, N., http://www.bertiedogs.com

INDEX